CONTENTS

plus additional local history throughout by Claude Fearns

Acknowledgements

Thanks to all who have contributed in any way, either stories or photos and memorabilia.
Thanks to Peak District National Park Authority for a contribution towards the costs.
Also thanks to Brian Rich, David and Mary Brindley, John and Wendy Mellor.

In several stories I have attempted to keep the dialect - I hope people can cope with this.

IN LONGNOR

Mary and Anne Grindey 1930s

Around Longnor

New Road Stores

Compiled by Sheila Hine
with additions by Claude Fearns

Front cover: Johnty Lownds at Boosley Grange.
He made the supreme sacrifice towards the end of the First World War
Back cover: At Boosley Grange. Back: Stuart Ryder, Eric Beresford, Joan Beresford, Joyce Sutton.
Front: John Beresford, Bobby Lownds, Norman Cope, Bernard Sutton

CHURNET VALLEY BOOKS
1 King Street, Leek, Staffordshire. ST13 5NW 01538 399033
www.leekbooks.co.uk
© Sheila Hine and Churnet Valley Books 2007
ISBN 978-1-904546 47 4

LONGNOR

LONGNOR is a small well-built market town, beautifully situated on a gentle declivity, bounded on the north by the Dove and on the south by the Manifold, and partakes of the hilly and verdant scenery characteristic of the northern parts of this county. The views from various places in its immediate vicinity are most picturesque and romantic. It is 6 miles south of Buxton, its post town, 10 north-east of Leek, and 153 north of London. It is one of the townships of the parish of Alstonfield, in North Totmonslow hundred, Leek union and county court district, Lichfield diocese, Stafford archdeaconry, and Alstonfield deanery, North Staffordshire. The church of St. Bartholomew is a plain structure, with a tower and 1 bell. It was rebuilt in 1780, and raised in height in 1812 so as to admit of galleries. The interior is neatly pewed. The living has had several augmentations, and is a parochial chapelry, including the chapelry of Quarnford, and townships of Hollins Clough, Heathy Lee and Fawfield Head above bridge. It is in the gift of the vicar of Alstonfield ; the annual value is £150 ; the Rev. George Frederick Williamson, M.A., is the incumbent. The Wesleyan Methodists have a chapel. In 1793 John Robinson bequeathed £196, secured on the Leek and Hassop turnpike road, and directed one-half of the interest (£9 16s.) to be paid to the Longnor schoolmaster, and the rest to the poor of Longnor and Heathy Lee. This bequest now yields about £2 10s. per annum. In 1794 Moses Charlesworth gave the interest of £20 to the Free school, which has fallen greatly into decay. In the churchyard is a stone, inscribed to the memory of William Billinge, an old soldier, who was born in a cornfield near Fawfield Head, and died, after having been at the siege of Gibraltar, in the battle of Ramillies, and other engagements, within 150 yards of the same spot, in 1791, aged 112 years. The township contains 793 acres, 775 of which are pasture, not more than 15 acres being arable land. Sir John Harper Crewe, Bart., is lord of the manor. The population in 1851 was 561. The market is on Tuesday. The interest of £20, left by Moses Charlesworth in 1794, and of £30 left by Mrs. Ann Collier in 1833, is distributed amongst poor widows. The latter also bequeathed the interest of £50 for schooling poor children. A church school has been established here by the Rev. William Buckwell, incumbent ; the scholars pay a small sum per week.

NAB END is a hamlet.

PRIVATE RESIDENTS.

Carlisle Rev. Charles Henry, A.K.S. [curate of Newtown & Reapsmoor]
Fernyhough Mrs
Williamson Rev. George Frederick, M.A. [incumbent]

COMMERCIAL.

Ball John, *Horse Shoe*, & shoemaker
Barlow Michael Blucher, linen & woollen draper
Belfield Isaac, baker & coal dealer
Bestwick John, tailor
Bradbury Robert & William, grocers
Bradbury Daniel, carpenter
Bradbury William, farmer, Edge top
Brewerton Edward, watchmaker
Charlesworth Moses, bone merchant & corn miller
Cundy Charles, butcher
Cundy James, butcher & shopkeeper
Deakeyne Hannah Charlotte & Ann (Misses), boarding & day school
Doughty Abel, shoemaker
Fowler William, *Cheshire Cheese*
Greaves George, saddle & harness maker

Gilman Isaac, *Butchers' Arms*, & shoemaker
Gilman Joseph, farmer, Gozzlecrofts
Goodwin George, surgeon
Gould Thomas, farmer
Grindey Thomas, *Crewe & Harpur Arms*, & cattle dealer
Grindey William, farmer & cattle dealer, Longnor edge
Harrison Ann (Mrs.), milliner & dressma
Harrison George, shoemaker, parish clerk & post office
Harrison John, shoemaker
Harrison Samuel, tailor
Harrison Thomas, tailor
Horobin Thomas, farmer, Nab end
Johnson Thomas, farmer, Nab end
Kidd William, shoemaker
Knowles Jane (Mrs.), baker
Lockett Thos. grocer, draper & druggist
Lomas Moses, shoemaker
Millward Joseph, farmer, Tunsted
Millward Joseph, joiner & cabinet maker
Millward Solomon, beer retailer & cabinet maker

Millward John, registrar of births & deaths for Longnor district, assistant overseer for Longnor & Heathy Lee, surveyor of Leek & Buxton & of Butterton Moor end turnpike roads, Fold end
Mottram Thomas, tailor
Needham Peter, farmer & cheese factor
Norton Andrew, druggist, grocer & draper
Oliver Robert Newton, farmer
Plant Mary (Mrs.), farmer, Nab end
Redfern Joseph, stonemason
Robinson Benjamin, *Red Bull*, & shopkeeper
Salt George, shoemaker
Smith George, wheelwright
Swindell Isaac, stonemason
Thirkettle Hen. saddle & harness maker
Wain James, farmer, Crofts
Wain John, grocer & provision dealer
Wain Joseph, farmer & foot postman
Wain Thomas, grocer
Wild John, farmer, Nab end
Wood John, cooper
Wood Thomas, farmer, Underhill

POST OFFICE.—George Harrison, postmaster. Letters arrive by foot messenger from Buxton at 10·30 a.m. & are dispatched at 4·30 p.m. except sunday

PUBLIC SCHOOLS :—
Free, John Welding, master *Sunday & Day*

CARRIERS :—
Joshua Knowles, to Leek, every wednesday, & to Sheffield on thursday, returning on saturday
James Smedley, wednesday, to Leek
Thomas Ball, ditto

From Kelly's Directory 1863

Ted Hall

I was born at the Royal Oak on Buxton Road in Leek, then in 1928 when I was 10, we moved up to the Moss Rose. There was a building on the yard, a garage and loose box with a good loft over. So my Dad and me kept some racing pigeons. The gable end was direct in line for pigeons coming north; so we whitewashed it so it could be seen, put a proper trap in and nest boxes.

There was no public water then, we had to cart drinking water from the spout down the road, but at the back of the house were some very large water butts about 10 foot deep. Anyhow one day there was no water and mother wanted to wash. They said *'It's funny there's been a lot of rain'*. So they got some from somewhere and she started, but there was no peace, she couldn't understand it. By then I'd gone off to school and Dad had a couple of lorries and they'd gone off as well. But by tea time there was a reception committee. Still no water! So Dad says, *'I'll ask Joe go up and have a look.'* So he got the ladder and went up. *'The's plenty o' watter in 'ere.'* *'Well, why have we no water then?'* Dad said. Joe replied, *'You'll 'ave stop*

At the Moss Rose Inn, 1930.
Harold Hall, Margaret, Ted, Ron and Elsie Hall, Dolly the pony, and Jack the dog.

1939 at the Moss Rose
Ted and Mary Hall, Ron Hall,
Mr and Mrs Hall.

them pigeons goin' on the roof.' It had washed the droppings down into the tanks till it had built up and blocked the outlet pipes. So Dad says, *'Tell Fred Barlow come... and bring a shovel.'* And he says to me, *'Are you going to do them, I'm too busy.'* In twenty-four hours, there were no pigeons left; I had to wring their necks, every one. We had pigeon pie and gave some away.

Some time later when I was working for Knowles butchers, a Mr Birch came in who we dealt with. He says *'Teddy, we've got a lot of white fantails, would you like a few?' 'Not a lot'* I hadn't forgotten the other episode. So he brought me a few up to Knowles; I thought perhaps if I kept them there, it'd be alright. Well they weren't very welcome, so I took them home. mother said *'What are you going to do with them?'* So I said *'I'll keep them in the loft and see what happens.'* They were very tame and mother softened. She said, *'Let them out for a bit, then shut them in again.'* So

Ted Hall at Hartington 1950s.

I did and they flew off next door and got up round his chimney. Bernard shouts down, *'Eh Teddy, the's some bloody white pigeons up on our roof, I dunner want 'em up there shittin'!'* 'Never mind, Mr Clowes, I'll fetch 'em in a bit.' I didn't want upset him, he could be hasty tempered. So I went round the back with a ladder to where the eaves were low and crept up to the chimney pretty handy, it was high enough. Luckily they were tame and I caught them one at a time; there was just one more and as I was reaching for that one, my foot slipped and I went down the roof on my backside thinking, *'I don't know what to do when I get to the gutter, I hope it dunner catch anywhere!'* Fortunately I'd been learning to jump and drop and I came sailing down the roof, the pigeons went up in the air and I landed on the lawn on my feet and bust me braces.

I went home. Mum says, *'Have you brought them fantails?' 'No, but me braces want mending.' 'Oh dear, what have you been up to? Perhaps they'll come down into the corn place.'* So the next day Bernard left the door open, they went in and he copped them quick. Mother found an owner for them straight away.

I left school when I was 14 and went to work for Knowles butchers in Derby Street in Leek. I'd been helping there for a while. I'll never forget my first day there; it was 1932 and foot and mouth had broken out, so we had to go and do a day's killing on a farm at Foston, at one of our customers called Mr Sant. The cattle couldn't be moved, so we killed and dressed them there and the beef went back to Leek the next day on a lorry. It was a wonderful farm and one of the animals that we killed was the best veal calf I've ever seen, a roan Shorthorn.

I was horseman at Knowles's as well, delivering round town; I did it on my own until I went in the army. The horses were two toppers, one was a half thoroughbred and the other a half hackney. They were perfect to drive and stand, never move a hoof.

One Monday night, when I was about 15, old Messina Knowles says *'Bring Polly up with Ginger tomorrow; I want you to fetch some lambs.'* We often only used one horse in the week and two at weekends. I wondered who was going with me. So we got the work done earlier and late afternoon he says *'Go put them in and get a piece of cord on Polly, she'll follow with the float.'* I asked *'Where are we going to?'* *'To Arthur Eardley's and Jack Fernihough's at Basford. Put both nets in, I'm going down on the bus.'* So I set off driving one and leading the other.

I got to Eardley's, where we sorted the lambs, loaded Polly and the float and netted it down. Messina says *'Leave her here, we'll take Ginger up to Fernihough's and load up.'* So we did and came back to pick Polly up, when Mr Eardley says *'Messina, there's these four young ewes, you'll take them won't you?'* *'There's no room in the float.'* *'They'll drive o'raight; I want 'em gone.'* *'Oh alright.'* And he turns the ewes off down the road. We get to the main road at Leekbrook, Messina walking in front to turn them towards Leek. I thought, *'I wonder when he's going to take over.'* Then I see a bus coming. He says *'Owd 'em 'ere, while this bus comes.'* So he stops the bus, then says *'I'm just goin' Wetley Rocks, you'll be o'raight.'* So I'm driving Ginger, leading Polly and four sheep walking in front. I did feel daft and thought *'If ever I land these lot up to the slaughterhouse in Cross Street, it'll be a miracle.'*

Well I got up there no bother, but the doors were shut; so I got off, left the horses standing and opened the doors. Meanwhile the sheep had wandered off up Fountain Street, so I ran after them and got them back; backed one mare in and unloaded, then the other, then turned the horses out. The old man never asked how I'd gone on, he never mentioned it.

When the war came, I signed up at the start and was called into the Infantry; I was a Militia Man and did various guard jobs around England. I didn't dislike army life; I became a corporal and spent quite a long time in Ireland. I was there when they arrested and locked up the first IRA people. We were on 72 hours stand to that weekend; it takes a bit of keeping awake.

There were 60 on detachment; one time we went to Cookestown, guarding a disused workhouse which was being made habitable for the Royal Fusiliers going over. It was to stop people setting fire to it. I was butchering there, some guard commanding and cooking. At that time they were in fear of a Russian invasion and four regiments went over. I was in the Hereford Regiment; there were Kings Shropshire Light Infantry, Royal Welsh Fusiliers and Third Mons.

The only time I looked like getting involved properly with fighting was when Narvic in north Norway was in danger of being taken over. We were allocated winter kit and got on a boat to go. We were away one and a half days at sea, then turned back; they'd lost or surrendered. So it was back to Ireland to guard the coast.

I then had several operations which weren't wholly successful and was reduced from A1 health, which ruled me out of active service, but put me in line for regimental butchering. I did a spell at Castle Wellan, so I've lived in a castle. The meat came from Newry. I learnt to break thoroughbred horses in there for racing. In the farmyard at the castle, there were big cattle sheds with deep bedding in, which were cleaned out once a year. The yearlings were turned in to tire them out. They'd sink in a bit, and you could ride them when they came out. And rats! The place was alive with them; I hated them to begin with; some were as big as cats. It was their sport on a Sunday morning, the men were out with their dogs and ferrets. There was a row of cottages and a rat hole in the wall, where they'd pop the ferret in; then they'd wait upstairs with a dog in the bedrooms and catch the rats; they could catch scores no trouble. I was cutting meat up in the cookhouse one time, reached up above a cupboard to get a tool and got hold of a big rat: I moved quick I can tell you.

There were some grand sights, I was intrigued at Cookestown. The main street was a mile long with another running parallel behind; that was about it. On market day, all the people came with their horses and Irish carts; the horses were put into stables and one side of the street was filled with the carts. They were biggish carts on small wheels and many had a litter of weaner pigs in, and though the shafts were on the floor and they weren't netted, I never saw one get out; they all lay fast asleep.

There was a tremendous amount of activity in the spring of the year, they'd come in with their travelling stallions down the main street. They were big clean-legged original Irish draughts. Halfway down the street was the Greyhound Inn, with a big opening in the middle where they went into the courtyard where there were stables and loose boxes. There was one a bit flighty, a good black 'un and as he turned in, he spun round, let go and kicked the window of the pub in!

It was such a different world; the carts were quite low to the floor with little iron wheels. I don't know how they made hay because I don't remember two fine days together, there was always a fine drizzle. They put poles up in the field and made a stack round it like a wigwam, then left it and come autumn time and a bit of decent weather, they'd come along with their flat cart and back up to the stack, undo the belly band, cock the shafts up so the back was touching the floor, put a rope on top and pull it onto the platform and away to go. It was goodish hay.

When I came out of the army, I heard that Mr Wilfred Palfreyman, butcher at Hartington had been taken ill. I'd heard about it from a chap I knew; he said *'Have you thought of going to Hartington, Mr Palfreyman wants to finish.'* This was on a Saturday in Buxton. So I got back to Leek, thought about it and decided to go and look. Of course there was no petrol, so I got on my bike and set off. I'd met Mr Palfreyman before, because on occasions, same as at Wakes time, he'd been down to Knowles for some topsides or the like to help him out.

I got there at teatime and said I'd heard he wanted to retire. He invited me in and the first thing he gets talking about is horses, we both shared a great interest. It took till about 10 o' clock to get past the horses, then he said *'I'm not selling the property, just the business, van, tools, fridges etc. Have a look round and put your value on it and we'll see if it's anywhere near mine.'*

Everything was good. *'Well,'* he said *'How much?'* and I said what I thought. *'You're a bit under.'* *'I expected you to say that, how much under?'* *'None much'* We were about fifteen quid out. *'Right, we'll have a deal; but I want you to do something for me. I want you to work for a month for nowt.'* This was the end of February 1944. *'At the end of March I shall have completed fifty years as butcher at Hartington.'* I said *'I'll do that gladly.'* *'And at the end of the month, you can spew it up if you decide you don't want it.'*

So then I said, *'It's time I went, it must be midnight.'* In the meantime there'd come about six inches of snow; you couldn't ride a bike down Mill Lane never mind over the moors. I couldn't ring 'cus we weren't on the phone in them days. There was nowt else for it but pop the bike on my shoulder and walk back to Leek; eleven miles. As I was getting towards the Moss Rose, I saw a light and as I was kicking snow off, mother came to the door. *'Where have you been till now?'* *'Coming!'* It had taken me five hours.

So we rented the shop and half the house. We didn't do any home slaughtering till 1954, everything had to be killed in a ministry licensed place while rationing was on, except one for yourself on your farm. So I went from Hartington to Ashbourne, three of us worked in Lou Allen's slaughterhouse. Piece's was another, Purdey's lads and Gregory's were workers there. There were two gangs of us; we used to go down Sunday morning and fetch the cattle up, from the Thursday

John Wood, Shawside, Upperhulme, cycling in the snow.

market, which had been left at The White Hart along Church Street. There were a lot of stables at the back of the pub and we met Fred Woolley and Arthur Chadwick there and took our allocation of cattle for slaughtering that morning out of the stables and walked them to the slaughterhouse. Three of us had 5 shillings for killing and dressing a beast and 9d for a sheep. You had to work fast; you could work your eyes and brains out till dinnertime and end up with about a quid.

On Monday again the same, but a bit later because what we'd killed on Sunday had to go out first; there was no hanging accommodation beyond a day's kill, they were only small places.

When rationing started, the ration was 1s 2d per person per week and meat was 1s 2d a pound, so a family with three children could have 5lb of beef a week. But in 1945, with a change of government, credit stopped. Thousands of tons of pork had been coming from Canada and beef from Argentina; it all stopped. It made a big difference; the first was the price of meat went up and then the ration was reduced; a double whammy! It worked out about a spoon of mince each! If I'd known what was going to happen, I wouldn't have taken the shop, it made life very difficult, especially trying to get a business going. We were hanging on hand to mouth. I did a lot of private pig killing, but there was no meat selling there - that was their own, they guarded it like gold. I was up at nights doing it; I'd kill and cut a pig up for 10s, in the early 50s one winter I did enough to buy a new Austin van.

I was very fortunate being a full blown journeyman; when I was 14 I could slaughter. That was in the days before captive bolts. Sheep and pigs were just stuck with a knife; on cattle you used a pole-axe, which was a little sledge hammer with a hollow spike with a hole in. As it entered the skull the bit of bone popped out. It knocked them out similar to the captive bolt, but it needed a clever eye and a steady hand. Old Messina Knowles was the best I've ever seen, a grand chap; I used to hold the cattle for him. He was a wizard and a very good butcher; his family came over from the French Revolution.

There's an art to sticking as well; I've killed hundreds, perhaps thousands, and never thought it was cruel. I'm a soft hearted man and the kinder you are to them the better, and the better the quality of the meat. When I was 16, captive bolts came in, then you needed a license which you couldn't have till you were 18, but I'd been killing since I was 13; lambs, sheep and little pigs.

When rationing finished in 1954 and I could kill my own stock, I bought at Ashbourne market on the first day. I'd made preparations, had the slaughter house tiled ready. Then I bought off local farmers, I was good friends with most of them. I bred and fed my own pigs and as I acquired land, I had my own lambs and some of my own beef too. One man let me have an acre to rent to start with, then I found myself accumulating; and I've always found room for a few horses, I've bred trotters for years. My wife helped in the business, and later my four daughters. We had a mobile shop which went out five days. We'd customers in Leek, Alstonefield, Wetton, over to Parwich, Buxton, Flash, Longnor, Earl Sterndale; a good trip round.

HARTINGTON

I used to try and be ahead of the job; I had the Meat Trades Journal every week and saw what changes were coming, like having no timber about during TT times when they were trying to eradicate TB. But I was helped out into doing that job. When we wanted to get a beast into the slaughterhouse from the lairage or clem shed, we popped a light chain round their head, if they'd got horns, you left one horn out, then it didn't hurt or strangle them, and there was a ring in the slaughter house which you pulled it through. Well I'd got two beautiful Galloways in; they were very fit, but it would have been easier to deal with some stags, one especially. I'd gone into the clem shed and Harry France, manager of Hart's Head Quarry and a good mate of mine had come. I said *'Can you give us a pull Harry?'* So he stood outside and I put the chain on. We had wooden stanchions and boskins and when he started pulling, the bullock cleared everything out. Harry shouts *'What's going on in there?'* *'I dunner know, but the bloody shed'll be down in a minute.'* He says *'How're you goin' on, I've been away from the pull, pulled back agen, away agen and back agen; I didn't know who was goin' through th' hole first.'*

When we looked in after, he said *'I've never seen such a mess in my life.'* The loft floor had come in as well. We had to clear it all out and put new concrete boskins in and iron gates. When the Inspector from the Midland Area Health Office came the next time he said, *'You're on the table before the meat!'*

Another time I was cratched. I'd bought a big black Hereford off a customer. He was a magnificent animal with big horns and he flipped his lid in the cattle wagon. As they dropped the ramp, he came flying out and smashed the lorry gates. He hadn't time to go in the clem shed, he ran up the yard, turned round and ran down the yard and hit the house head on. Good job there wasn't a window there. That mesmerised him a bit, he went back up the yard slower, saw the open door, went in and I didn't half shut it quick. He gave it some hammer. This was Saturday morning and later on after tea Mary said, *'What if some kids should come in, I think you should get him killed.'* There were some courting couples sometimes came up the yard for a cuddle; so I thought that sounded sensible.

So I thought *'I'm not going in there on my own, I'll go down to the yard gate and see if there's anybody about.'* Jack Salt was there. *'Can you spare a minute to stand at the lairage door; I've got an upset bullock.'* So I quietly opened the door and crept in, he was standing at the other end and as I made my way to open the other door, he wakened up and came after me. I beat him, jumped up on a boskin and into the cratch. Every time I moved my feet, he was trying to get at me. Jack shouted, *'What shall I do Ted?'* *'Slip down to Joe Brindley, Walter'll be finished milking. Bring a lorry rope and make a noose and in the slaughterhouse you'll find a long arm, a pole with a hook on.'* So they did and sneaked the long arm with the noose on into the shed; I'd come along the cratch towards them and kept rattlin' me feet to keep his attention, so they didn't have to open the door much. So quietly, quietly we managed to get in position; he's goin' mad at me into the bottom of the cratch. I got the rope and dropped it over his horns and they pulled him. There was a hook they tied off to. *'What now?'* They said. I replied, *'We're one man short.'* Just then the copper comes up; Reg Calloway. *'What's goin' on up 'ere?'* *'The right man, just in time.'* *'Why, what's up?'* We'd still got the chain to pull in, even though by then we'd got a stunning pen. So to hedge our bets we managed to get the chain on him, one horn in, one out and as Reg pulled him in to the slaughterhouse, the others paid him off a bit at a time. He killed out fine, not a mark on him.

A local dish I came across was 'hackin'. I was at Brund and we'd killed a very good pig; it was 22 score (440 lbs), the fat bacon was 4 inches deep. The fat was saved off the entrails; that was called the 'midgeon', and I was told it made the best hackin. Then there was the leaf fat from inside the bacon and any spare fat. It was all cut up and rendered. Then you got the scratchings, that was the residue. That was minced or chopped. Meanwhile the liver and heart had been cooked and minced. It was all mixed up together with some seasoning and cooked in a big cloth and finished off in a big roasting tin. Then you could cut it and eat it; it was damn good. I'd never come across it till I met the Critchlow family.

I used to go to the Higg Lane blacksmith near Rewlach. He was Bill Mellor, brother of Albert at Longnor who had the great trotting horse, Neponset. He was a grand chap and learnt me a lot of things. He'd make a set of bevelled shoes; I had some on a colt I showed at Leek horse sale; it made him pick his feet up. And he showed me the secret of horse whispering years ago.

My brother in law, Bill Hulme and me used to go Market Drayton Dirty Fair, buying Welsh Cobs, colts usually. I'd have two; break 'em in and take 'em Leek Horse Sale. I took one that I'd started breaking to have it shod. I'd never touched its feet. *'What 'ave you got, a colt?'* *'No, a filly.'* It was a little hovel. He says, *'Back her in.'* So he goes round and tries her feet and she's well behaved till he gets to the off hind, when she let go and kicked the wall behind. *'Well I'll be damned, bring her out side.'* He said *'And put this rope on her halter end.'* We went into the field opposite where Mr Salt's office was. He got himself a long twig with a few leaves on the end, put her out on the rope and waved the stick. She went round a few times. Then he got a pull strap which goes through a keeper then a buckle. *'Just owd 'er yed.'* He picked her front foot up and slipped it onto the bottom part of her leg, tied the remaining strap round the top of her leg and fastened it up - she's on three legs. *'Right.'* He says *'I don't know what'll happen, I'll go behind.'* She started going on three legs, realised she wasn't going anywhere so settled down going in a circle on three legs. He says *'Dus know Ted, we'en won.'* He took the strap off and she never ever looked like kicking again.

Arthur Gee Snr at Ridge Farm 1931

Anne Thompson at Dale Farm in the Manifold Valley.

The Observer Corps at Hartington. The three posts of the N Group, Hartington, Rushton and Ipstones.

Stuart Gilman

My family were Gilman's Tailors in the market place at Longnor. Grandad started the business in the early part of the 1900s. There was a shop downstairs which sold clothes; ladies' clothes, hosiery, gents' clothes, anything you wanted.

Dad took over when Grandad died, about 1939. He carried on making suits and corduroy trousers for farm workers; he'd learnt off Grandad. He employed a bit of labour to help; Fred Wardle who used keep the Horseshoe used come and do a couple of hours tailoring in the afternoon, Monday to Friday.

Dad did some farming at Islington Farm on the Buxton road and spent his afternoons tailoring. Great-grandad Findlow had bought some land at Islington and built a house on it and went on from there. They milked 7 or 8 cows by hand; in the summertime they were milked in the fields. So morning and night was farming and the shop after dinner. He'd have an order in for a suit, so cut it out and the next afternoon, sew it all up.

I've been here at Daisy Knowle for 50 years; Dad came here after selling Islington house but he kept the land to put with this. He finished with the shop in 1952 when his mother died and the rest of his family wanted their shares out; he had 7 brothers and sisters.

We carried on farming and making cheesecloths. We had that job for a while. Special cloths came in flat packs. Each one was cut out separate but wanted sewing up at an angle, so they had to be marked and sewn in that way to fit the cheese mould. We got ¹/₂d each which went up to 1d. So in the 1950s you sewed up 240 to get £1. They went to three cheese factories, Reapsmoor, Glutton Bridge and Rowsley. Jack Sutton was the boss over them; he brought the stuff to us, then distributed the sewn up cloths. We did it for years; it fitted in with the farm work. If there was a purge on, we had to sit up all night. Dad had brought the treadle machines here to work with. Me or Mum and Dad made them, one marking and one making up.

Opposite Islington farm, what is now known as Islington Villas, used to be the Lodging house. Years ago, tramps would stay there for a night. I remember as a child seeing an old man from Hollinsclough Moor curled up asleep on the roadside agen the door in a morning. He'd been drinking in Longnor. You often heard them carrying on at night on their way home.

Islington on the Buxton Road at Longnor.

Dennis Birch

My Grandad, Joseph Birch lived at Digmer Farm, Hartington and my Mum and Dad were living there when I came along in 1929. Then my Dad took a farm at Brund, he rented it from the Grindon family at Warslow. It was £120 a year for 72¹/₂ acre. I was 2 or 3 at the time. We milked cows; hand-milking; then we had a milking machine put in and it milked 2 cows at once with units, that's buckets. That milked 12 cows, the others 'ad be milked by hand, there was no airline to them, it was over the road. Me and our David could milk by hand.

We used do all th' work wi' horses, we 'ad 2 cart horses, Bonnie and Queenie. I used do all th' work wi' them when I left school at 14. I did chain harrowin', muck cartin'; load all th' muck be 'and, put it all out inter 'eaps, then go back an' spread it by 'and. I did all that at 14. It were all right, we'd nowt else 'ad we, but I'd sooner 'ave a tractor. I ploughed a field with 2 horses; I was only a lad, made a good job. We used grow cabbage and kale, potatoes and oats.

In 1947, we 'ad a brand new tractor, a David Brown. Belfields 'ad the first one round here, an owd Fordson; they were contractors up Sheen Lane, but we were the first farmers I think. They did discin' an' corn cuttin', we thought it was wonderful; we didn't want th' horses any more. Me Dad sold one, but we kept th'other for quite a while.

Belfields used plough for me Dad an' disc for 'im at start and cut the corn. As years went on, Mr Woolley at Cronkston lent us his discs and his binder and we used build corn stacks an' 'ave Ron Rogers to thrash it. Him an' 'is brother Ivan used come with threshin' box and baler. They used thrash for us an' Hilda and George next door and Jim, their dad; we all used 'elp one another.

We used take the corn to Brund Mill, where they dried it and ground it, we fed the straw to the cows. We 'ad all this corn in bags, some was not very good. There were 4 bags across the back of the threshin' box; one was best quality, then second best, third was goin' worse an' fourth was like bird seed and bits. Wonderful thing though, thrashin'. I used be on top o'th thrashin' drum, feedin' it; I used love it. Cut the sheaves, spread it and put it through. Two Rogers brothers, me an' me brother, Jim from next door and Dad. We 'ad about six stacks; then we 'ad stack all the straw up as 'ad been baled.

Brund Mill

I can't remember Dad thatchin' 'is stacks, but owd Jim from next door used go up Arbage (Herbage) Barn an' mow rushes with scythe an' tie 'em up in battens, bring 'em back an' thatch 'is stacks. 'E were good; 'e'd come back with a great trailer load; 'is stacks were wonderful, you never saw a job like it.

Dad's cousin, Harold Birch had the mill at Brund and used do the corn for people round. Keith Morris from Sheen used work for 'im and I spent an 'our with 'im now an' then cus 'e were my mate. On the side of the road, you stopped your wagon and a chain hung down, which you hooked round the top of the bag and up it went into the mill. There was a big fire with grids on top with little holes through and 'e 'ad like a brush stail with a board on an' 'e used rake it, these oats over top o' these grids to dry it. I was up there one mornin', it was hot; they were very small 'oles, you could see the fire through and every so often, you 'ad rake it. Then it went through the grindin' stones, the water drove them.

Harold was a good joiner as well, 'e could make anythin' - cart wheels and 'e made us a corner cupboard. If you 'ad a bent circular saw blade, 'e could straighten it an' cut new teeth in the blade. Like new, when 'e'd done it. 'E made a car into a lorry, an old Austin 12, cut the back off an' put a fresh body on it. Used it for cartin' wood an' stuff about. 'E 'ad a car as well. When 'e'd done this little truck, 'e went to Newcastle an' back with it an' do you know it was good on petrol, it used a gallon and three quarters all but an egg-cup full; 'e'd measured it out.

Dad took the milk to th' cheese factory at Hartington every day an' dropped us off and we went to school and then 'e went drivin' a lorry all day for 'is brother, cartin' coal from Hartington station. Uncle Charlie couldn't drive, so me Dad drove it an' all 'e got was 'e never 'ad to buy any coal; Uncle Charlie give 'im the coal for 12 months. And 'e used the lorry for taking the milk with, we went to school in it and kept it in a shed at Brund. Then 'e 'ad come back an' do 'is work at night. But 'e 'ad a man workin' for 'im, Charlie Mellor from School Clough, Newtown. So me mother an' Charlie did the work while me Dad were gone.

After school, we went Grandad's an' Dad picked us up an' brought us 'ome. Uncle Charlie lived with Grandad at Digmer.

Dad died in 1961 and we 'ad come out next Lady Day, 25th March. So me an' David 'ad to do the farm up so they couldn't claim compensation off us. Then we went up to Fold Farm at Sheen; Dad 'ad bought that off 'is brothers, Uncle Joe and Uncle Charlie, 46 acres. So we'd got that and 72$\frac{1}{2}$ acre an' then me an' David bought 22 acres the other side of Hartington off Uncle. We 'ad three lots till we 'ad come out of Brund, so then

Uncle Joe Birch

we'd got 46 an' 22. We thought that's not enough for two families, we were both married then; so we got a lorry. It was 1962; people didn't know us, so we went cartin' corn for Staffordshire Farmers. We got 15 shillings a ton for cartin' corn; we picked it up at the warehouse in Ashbourne and took it to farms. We both went, in between milkin', we soon 'ad it off, two of us.

Then we got friendly with a man, Bill Seward from Duckmanton near Bolsover and 'e found us some people to buy hay and straw off. We got goin' then, 'e told 'em we were right an' straight, they'd no need t' be frightened of sellin' us stuff. It went like mad, one tells another, don't they? We were goin' that well, we couldna' cope wi' one wagon, we 'ad t'ave another. So we bought Stead's wagon from up Flash for £650 an' David went on silage, it was a tipper. He had to cut silage with a hay knife and fork it onto the lorry; 8 tons, then go an' tip it. He mauled hissel' to death; I 'ad go with 'im sometimes t' 'elp 'im load. One load a day if the orders were in and if 'e 'adn't got a load o' silage, 'e stayed at 'ome ter catch up with the work.

'E made an extension for the back of the tipper, 3 foot long, then 'e could cart hay and straw on it as well; 'e'd get 5 or 6 tons on with a rack over the cab as well. We've shifted tons and tons of stuff, nobody knows. 328 bales on mine one day, 9 high with a 6 foot cab rack and 2 foot on the back. All loaded and stacked by hand, put on with forks!

Anyway, we got fed up of loadin' by 'and, so we bought a tractor off Colin Grindey with a loader on and took that down there to Camm's at Retford; Camm's Farmers Ltd; they let

Dennis Birch with crop sprayer and Super Cropmaster tractor.

us keep it in a buildin'. This was for loadin' pea silage; they made it for us in a big yard; so David was alright then, loadin' with this tractor with a fork on. I didn't 'ave go then. Some farmers went with 'im to 'elp load when it was by 'and.

We'd got a load of hay on for this man at Buxton one night, it were dark, we were late, both of us. I'd got a rack over the cab, right to the front. We 'ad come back an' milk then. Well, where 'e wanted me to go, I wanted to draw up to the pickin' 'ole, an' throw it off at the front. Oh no, 'e wouldn't let me do that; I'd got draw down an' back up. Well, there was a flash like lightenin', down came the electric wires; milkin' machine stopped. 'E 'ad get 'lectric Board out that time o' night. *'It's my own fault,'* he said. *'I should have let you done what you wanted.'* I could 'ave seen with my lights, then, where I was goin'.

When we were deliverin' corn once, we were in a steep yard; dropped 'is corn off an' couldn't get out. We 'ad to shift all the corn from the front onto the back axle to get out.

We carted sugar beet pulp from the sugar factories; David used cart loose pulp on the tipper; 'e 'ad shovel it onter his lorry, an' I used cart bags on the flat wagon. I'd go down to Newark an' put 8 ton o' bags on by 'and. They used come down a rubber conveyor belt an' I 'ad stack 'em; 80 lb paper bags. If it rained, we 'ad sheet up. The lad at the sugar factory said to me, 'You're the best man as comes 'ere, you are; the's nobody as can stack bags as quick as you and make as good a job!' I were proud o' that.

Another thing we did was contract balin'. David did it all first; we had the first baler in 1957, then in 1959, we 'ad 'ave another, we were that busy. We were both contract baling all round Sheen, Hartington, Longnor, all the local villages through the 1960s. Then people started gettin' their own balers and it died down.

You'd be doin' the milkin', goin' on the lorry, comin' back an' somebody wants some balin' doin'. It was quiet on the lorries at that time though, winter was the busy time; there was a lot of pressure on sometimes.

Joyce Perkin

I was born in February 1930 at East View, Newtown. My Dad was Isaac Gee and my Mum, Sarah Elizabeth Sutton from Pyeclough. They farmed, milking about 9 cows.

I can remember walking to Newtown school and meeting Old Peg Legs going into Shawfield Wood for sticks without his legs. He was only little when he'd got no legs on, he just had some bags round his stumps and shuffled about. His little house was not far from the wood. He also had a little donkey and went off on it with his wooden legs on.

One bad winter, in wartime, I think 1940, all the trees were pulled down with the weight of icicles and branches were breaking off, they were that heavy. Grandad Gee had died and his body lay in the house for ten days; it was too bad to bury him, the ground would be frozen and the roads were blocked, no-one could get.

There was a baby being born at Fleet Green, Joan Cundy and no-one could get. Nurse Wheeldon from Longnor had to come and the policeman, Sergeant Davenport and Mr Thompson had to carry her, holding her arms up over the drifts of snow. They couldn't find their way, they were lost, but we'd never drawn our blackout properly and a light was showing which drew them to us. Sergeant Davenport knocked on the door, *'Where's your blackout, Isaac?'* he said. They stopped a while to rest and have a cup of tea, Nurse Wheeldon was exhausted and there was still about three quarters of a mile to go up Lady Edge and then down the fields.

They carried on and the baby was safely delivered. Dad left a lantern out all night to guide them back. He was told off in a jokey way for breaching the blackout and warned not to let it happen again.

I met Jack Perkin when I worked at Tattons Mill at Upperhulme; I was fabric finishing there. We had some rough journeys getting there on the bus in winter. Jack was in the army, doing his two years National Service after the war. He came from Harpurs End. When he finished in the army, he worked at the dyehouse for a bit, then went in the quarry, I think it was Dowlow. Then, when the keeper for the Harpur-Crewe estate left, Jack applied for the job and got it. It was a big area, something like 2,000 acres, the Warslow Moors Estate and covering Flash area.

We lived then at Hayes Head, Shawfields, Newtown, which actually was just below Mum and Dad's farm. We called it Keepers Cottage. We went there in '55 and left in '86.

Jack's biggest job was catching foxes and crows, and sometimes stoats and weasels. They had fox shoots and on a moonlight night, he used sit in the pickin' 'ole down the yard and shoot them when they came in the moonlight.

He had to catch poachers; there were a lot in those days after the grouse and it could be a dangerous job, but he rarely seemed to have trouble with them when he took their guns. I've got no end of letters of when he went to court with poachers. He became a Special Constable and could catch them better then. He used to go on his motor-bike with his uniform on and put his old army coat on top and his hat in a bag and go like that and when he saw poachers, he would drive past them and throw his coat off and put his police hat on and come back and they wondered where he had come from.

The grouse-shooting season was from August to December with sometimes a rough shoot for pheasants and the like. The first shoot of the season was the Glorious 12th of August. They used to come back to our house for lunch, which I'd get for them.There used to be 8 guns and sometimes friends or wives came along too. Mr Harpur-Crewe - we knew him as Mr Charles - was nice, he used to come into the kitchen talking to us. He used to stop down at Warslow Hall.

Newtown School 1926. Teacher Miss Marion Carrington, Assistant Miss Florence Gilman. From *Story of Newtown* by J. Nichol.
BACK: Miss Florrie Gilman, Ann Bradbury Shining Ford, Winnie Ball Holly Grove, Agnes Riley Badgers Croft, Harriet Gee Upper Fleet Green, Mary Milward Shawfield, Rose Mellor Newhouse, Nellie Bradbury Shawfield.
2ND: Jack Woolley The Bank, George Bradbury Shawfield, John Oliver Newtown, Jimmy Ball Holly Grove, Raymond Gregory Hall Hill, Colin Lownds Boosley, George Mellor Newhouse, Isaac Gee Upper Fleet Green.
3RD: Richard Riley Badgers Croft, Rachel Riley Badgers Croft, Jane Cantrell Barrow Sitch, Louise Mellor Newhouse, Mattie Mellor Newhouse, Toddy Bradbury Shining Ford, Annie Ball Noon Sun, Mona Bradbury The Slack, Gwen Haywood Round Knowle, Mary Bradbury Shining Ford.
4TH: Stanley Gregory Hall Hill, Dorothy Webster Oxbatch, Miriam Prince The Lane, Fanny Riley Badgers Croft, Phyllis Ball Holly Grove.
FRONT: Jack Beresford The Hocker, John Cantrell Barrow Sitch, Tom Riley Badgers Croft, Herbert Mellor Newhouse, Gilbert Lownds Boosley, Matthew Beresford The Hocker, Charlie Mellor Newhouse.

..... and more country children.

Nancy and John Bonsall 1924

John Gilman and David Bradbury at Lapwing Farm 1948

Jack with a fawn at Shawfield Wood.

Jack Perkin and
George Bradbury
going foxing, 1960.

Mum at
Pyeclough.

Dad (Isaac Gee) in Home Guard.

Jack with Spider 1958.

Jack as a Special around 1960.

Dad thatching a stack.

Joyce and Jack.

Captain Haslam
1960s.

Pyeclough 1930s.

Mr Charles Harpur-Crewe with Jack and son Malcolm

Fetching drinking water from off the moor across
Lady Edge with my sister Joan and a friend.

Mum and Dad (Gee).

The family
haymaking, and
Captain Haslam.

Haymaking at Boosley Grange

Fred Lownds taking the milk to the Cheese factory 1936.

Prince Mellor

I remember as a child at School Clough in wartime, walking to Longnor School every day with gas masks. There was gas mask drill in the paddock next to the vicarage. We could be lying on our faces or crawling about under trees. We had to buy a waterproof case to carry it in; the cardboard boxes would soon have perished.

The bombing raids were very frightening, if they came close we would go down the cellar to shelter. There were three big bombs dropped near here; one next to The Ferns, one next to School Clough and one next to Fawfieldhead. They were what they called 1,000 pounders. Shrapnel flew right over School Clough House to the other side; you could find pieces as big as your hand, ragged and sharp. My sister was standing in Keeling's doorway, just up the road at Summerseat and she saw them drop even though it was night-time. The ground shook and it cracked the gable-end of The Ferns house.

The craters were very big and we had to fill them in. Some people threw rubbish in to help fill them and I remember one lad coming from Longnor picking bottles out to take back to the pubs for 2d each. All the soil was there, but it was all spade work, no tractors then; it took days and days spading it in. Eventually the job was finished and I don't think you could tell where they were now.

Prince Mellor.

I also remember counting our own planes one day going over high up. 157 Flying Fortresses in batches, going out bombing.

An article in a farming paper said that the electric fence was invented in New Zealand around 1950. This prompted me to write a letter in reply recalling an incident when I was at school around 1940. The farmer next to the school had one, it was thick wire then and I remember testing it for curiosity with an old penny. As I touched the wire, the shock knocked me down on my back. But I went back to the school sports and won the 100 yard race.

THE FEARNS: MASTER FORGERS (Claude)

In 1797, on the Pembrokeshire coast, three ships appeared on the horizon. They were being watched carefully by a retired sea- captain who had built himself a lookout post on one of the hills. The ships were flying the British colours, but the captain thought that there was something wrong with them, He was watching the method of sail, they were tacking against the wind about two miles off-shore, when he suddenly realised that they were three French ships, Men of War. He alerted the local town that they were being invaded, but the Militia were at Cardigan, some 40 miles away. A rider was sent for them immediately.

In the meantime, the French were coming into port and as they landed, they were met by the ladies of the town with jars of old cider. Now the French were 'dry' ships, meaning they carried no alcohol aboard and seeing the ladies so friendly with their jars of cider, they decided to try it and thinking it was poor quality wine, they drank their fill.

The consequences were that they were soon legless, except for a few who didn't drink as much and a gang of these went pillaging. They met up with the blacksmith's wife, who managed to kill three of them; perhaps made easier because they had been drinking.

There were no men in town at all; they were hiding in the hills, waiting to swoop back as the Militia arrived. Had they stayed in town and there had been a battle, they could have been wiped out by the better armed French marines. It was left to the women to do the best they could. It may be said that they left the women to their fate at the hands of the Frenchmen, but had the men stayed and been killed, the raping and pillaging would have gone on anyhow.

The Militia arrived before the Frenchmen had recovered from their heavy cider drinking; not being used to it. So they were soon overpowered, taken prisoner and their ships impounded. Their mission to get the Welsh to rise against the English was a total failure.

The English realised that all their money was in the form of gold - the French had been collecting, so the British government decided that gold would be replaced by paper money.

Now people had never seen paper money before, so they had no idea when it was exchanged for their gold if it was genuine or not. This led the Fearns family of Bottomhouse to take advantage and produce their counterfeit money. To launder the money, they would go to markets and buy cattle, take them home and grow them for a week or two, then send them to a different market to draw real cash. They also worked on people's greed; the Bank of England paid £1 paper money for a sovereign. The Fearns would give two forged notes for a sovereign.

As the money passed around, it lifted the local economy. But the Fearns got greedy; they bought a pony and cart and employed a Mr Mellor to travel round exchanging fake money. He got caught at Chester and once caught, he squealed like a pig, telling the detectives all he knew about the Fearns family. The police raided the premises at Bottomhouse, but they found nothing, so Detective Nadin, the Manchester thief-taker was summoned to the area to sort it out.

Nadin stayed at the Fearns' pub overnight disguised as a pedlar along with a constable in disguise. They managed to get into George Fearns confidence by showing him some forged money of their own, to which he said it was a poor sample and he could get better stuff. Which he did, and it led to his arrest with the counterfeit goods on him. He was committed to the county gaol at Stafford, the trial took place in July 1801 and in due course he was sentenced to death and was hung.

They had also been making counterfeit coins and had kept the 'dies' hidden in the thatch of a stack on a farm some fields away from their pub, which was on the crossroads on the old road which ran above the current main road from Leek to Ashbourne.

George was my great, great, great uncle and during a discussion about the story once, a man thought it was very funny that some of my relations had been caught for forgery until I pointed out that it was a 'Mellor' who had 'shopped' them - whose name he shared.

Jim Finney

The Finney family were at Harley Grange, near Earl Sterndale. My Grandfather, William married Alice Hodgkinson from Flagg Hall, in Manchester Cathedral in 1864. They had a large family of eight children. Uncle Tom went to Edinburgh University and became a doctor and was then employed by a mining company in Pontypridd, South Wales amongst the mining

Uncle Tom with gundogs at Belfield House.

community. He once lanced some boils on my neck - you don't forget that.

Grandfather had been ill for some time; he'd got a very bad leg which he'd injured horse riding and he died in 1883. Grandma stayed on the farm with some of the sons for a while and my father, Charles Fielding Finney left the farm in 1899 to go to Cawlow Farm, Hulme End. He married and they had two boys, Wilshaw and Fielding, my half brothers, who went to Australia.

Father lost his wife in childbirth with their third child in 1903 and married my mother, Bertha Hambleton from Heathy Roods, Butterton in 1906. I was born in 1916 and already had a brother and sister, Ann and John; I was the youngest and I was born at Herbage Farm at the top of Elkstones, where they had moved to.

There were stories of ghosts at Herbage but I never saw anything, perhaps I was too young. Over certain years, there seemed to be happenings, then it was quiet. My sister, Ann, said she wakened up one morning and saw a man at her bedside and his face was all scarred like someone with smallpox. And a black dog followed Dad home from the pub, The Cock at Elkstones.

One day, mother had been asleep on the sofa by the old range and when she woke up, there was a figure standing in front of the fire with very old-fashioned clothing on, knee britches and that. Then it was gone. They weren't bothered about these things. One early spring evening, the light was fading and one cat, when it was quiet liked to just have a look on the table, to see if there were any scraps. Mother was sitting on the sofa - all at once this cat sprang up onto the table, sprang off and bolted. The stairs were creaking, but there was no-one there.

Dad just out of the hayfield, a pork butcher from Bakewell ? Mr Simpson, and postman John Finney.

In 1925, Herbage was sold and we moved to Belfield House, Newtown. From Top House past Shining Ford is Coalpit Lane and there are the remains of a little stone quarry which the old roadmen used. I remember them with their wheelbarrow, spade and brush and scythes, trimming the roadsides in summer - no sign of tarmac then. I used to bike a lot; when there'd been a lot of heavy horses over, stone was kicking up everywhere, terrible to ride on.

Jim Finney at Belfield House.

My sister Anne on the road near Heath House with Mrs Nelson (mounted) from Lower Boothlow.

Johnny Bradbury lived just off the lane, we called him Johnny Barrersytch; the place is Barrow Sytch. I knocked about with John Berrisford and we used to tease him. We were once helping him haymaking, rakin' up and he called us for dinner. I'd called him something rude and when we went in, he came for me with a big knife, *'Now, what did you call me?'* I ran, jumped up on a wall and it collapsed. He said he wasn't getting many eggs, so we fastened some papers on some of the hens - he'd get none after that. Another time, we put some water in his oil lamp and we sat, hiding, listening and he was cossin' because he couldn't get it to go.

One night we were passing Shining Ford, it was with John again and it was a lovely moonlit night, a Saturday, and Mrs Bradbury, a lovely lady, had put her chairs outside while she was cleaning up ready for Sunday. We had our old dog with us and it had caught a rabbit and killed

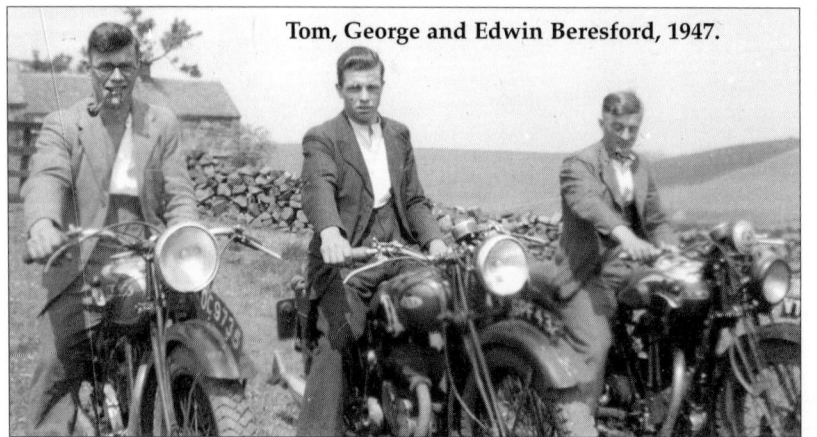

Tom, George and Edwin Beresford, 1947.

it. So we got the idea and put it on the seat of one of the chairs. Her daughter, Mary went to fetch the chairs in and when she saw the rabbit, she let out such a squeal. We were hiding under the wall again listening. In October 1933, we moved to Limerick Farm, Longsdon.

Bernard Brown

I was headmaster at Sheen School for 12 years until it closed. I went for the interview in November; it was snowing like mad. There were four other candidates for the job and I was the only one who got through, the others got stuck in various places. There was a chap from Stafford got through to do the interviewing; he said, *'We mustn't just have Mr Brown, because the other people haven't had a fair chance.'* The governors said, *'They've had as much chance as him- he's our man, he's the one who's got here; if the others can't get here for an interview, they wunner get here t' teach'.*

It came out in conversation that I was married to a Critchlow; I wonder if that helped me get the job! I remember the interview was in the vicar's study and the governors had come along in their wellies with muck and snow on and when they crossed their legs, I could see the snow melting and dripping off, and puddles developing on the vicar's carpet.

One time, there was a teachers' strike and I wouldn't go on strike and the pickets were going round to the schools where people were still working. I had a word with Mr Critchlow at the Manor. He said, *'Any trouble Mr Brown and we'll have the lads out'.* That was the tug of war team; there were three of his lads in it and one or two of the neighbours' lads. *'You can let it be known that the TOW team will come to your rescue, that'll perhaps keep them away.'* So we let it be known and they never did come.

I was the Junior teacher, Miss Philp, the vicar's daughter was the Infant teacher, Mrs Bates the ancillary assistant, Irene Gould, one of the dinner ladies, Mrs Simpson brought the dinners from Warslow and May Critchlow, caretaker - later it was Mrs Gould. At one stage, three of the children were my own - three were the dinner ladies and two were Mrs Bates'; that's 8 of the children belonged to three of the staff. We were trying to keep ourselves in a job and it was easier to take my children to school with me than for my wife to walk them to school and back at Rushton. We'd only the one car, and of course Rushton had plenty of children and was not threatened with closure.

A tradition was when we had a new arrival; Miss Philp would get the previous arrival to take them on a tour of the school. So round they went, pretending that it was a big place - into the infants' room, then *'this is the junior room, and this is the hall where you have your dinner and sing; I'll take you and show you the toilets'.* You had to go across the yard, they were chemical toilets. Then Herbert came back with Christopher. *'Now Christopher, when you've been to the toilet, you must wash your hands. Come into the cloakroom and I'll show you the wash basins. Can you see these two taps - one says C for cold and the other says H for warm'.*

I enjoyed my time there, they were lovely children. One day we were reading from the Bible the story of Jesus walking on the water. The disciples had been fishing all night and *'Peter cast his fisherman's coat about him for he was naked'.* Louise read it - *'Peter cast his fisherman's coat about him cus he was knackered.'* *'No, no naked, he wasn't knackered!'* I said; then John shouted, *"E would be Mr Brown, dunner ferget 'e'd bin fishin' o nate'.*

Les Armitt in the hayfield at Brund, 1960s.

BACK: Susan Cantrell, Margaret Deaville, Mary Cope, Mary Critchlow, Pat Thompson,
Ron Blackhurst, Tony Hayward,Paul Goodwin, David Wood, Myrtle Critchlow, Malcolm Gould.
FRONT: Michael Morson, Dilys Critchlow, Brenda Critchlow, Grenthal Hartley, Arthur Morson,
Peter Howson, Lillian Shann.

Sheen School late 1960s with Bernard Brown. BACK: John Critchlow, Chris Belfield, George Critchlow,
Anne Oliver, Herbert Shann, Susan Belfield, Janet Birch, Terence Birch.
FRONT: Beverly Howson, Carol Birch, Linda Birch, Anne Critchlow, Tracy Goodwin.

THE MEN OF LONGNOR (Claude)

Around 1572, John Harpur enclosed Brownspit, Heath House and Fawside, thus cutting off the men of Longnor from their ancient grazing rights at Fawfieldhead, known as 'The Hills'.

The first winter, they used the fodder up as normal, but the next year, not being able to send the cattle onto the common for grazing; they had to graze their meadows off. Come autumn, no grass, no hay, nothing for the winter. So most of the cattle had to be killed off, leaving the people of Longnor without milk and cheese and when they were gone, no meat either.

This dispute between John Harpur and the residents became violent and John sent for the Militia to put down the rebellion. But someone from the government refused to send the Militia because of heavy bloodshed at a previous uprising. Instead, they sent an adjudicator to hear both sides. John Harpur claimed that the men of Longnor had enough ground in Longnor itself. They, in turn said they had not and had always had grazing rights over the 300 acres of the common. The adjudicator, in his wisdom, to appease both sides, gave 200 acres to John Harpur and 100 acres to the men of Longnor in perpetuity. This is in the Longnor Wood area.

Maurice Lowe

THE SHIRLEYS OF REWLACH: We have records of Shirleys at Rewlach going back to the 1600s - John Shirley. His grandson John married Mary Johnson of Boothlow. She heard one of John Wesley's preachers in Longnor square and was inspired to start a group at Rewlach Farm, the start of Methodism at Rewlach. The chapel was built around 1849, the Shirley family gave the land and a note from William Shirley's diary states that it was built for £100 and was free from debt because most of the labour was given.

I was born at the Holmes Farm and attended the chapel regularly until it was held for one Sunday a month during the summer, which was about 20 years ago, when we started to go to Longnor. Both chapels have since closed. Rewlach Chapel was part of the Wetton and Longnor Circuit and my father, George Lowe, preached there and in the circuit. There was a minister at Wetton, the house next to the chapel there is still called The Manse. There were 13 chapels in the 1950s until it was broken up and they went to different circuits, this end to the Buxton Circuit, Warslow and Hartington to Leek; Alstonefield and Wetton to Ashbourne.

Although there were perhaps only 4 or 5 families who attended, they were large families and with their workers, the chapel would be full. My main memory as a child was when the Reverend Summers was at Wetton. He held monthly rallies at various chapels and quite a few at Rewlach. The place was always full and he played a piano-accordion. He made a big impression on me; he was forthright and sought to bring life back into the country chapels.

Another preacher that I respected was Harry Bailey, a real gentleman. Hector Peacock was full of fun, an extrovert. One of his sayings was, *'Let the dog see the rabbit'*. Then there was Mr Laurence, who we as children found long-winded and Walter Cundy. Happy days!

There was a tiny little chapel at Kirkham Yard, Reapsmoor, a little building on the side. One of my last memories as a child was of my father preaching at the harvest festival there. He sat down on the seat in the pulpit and it collapsed.

Camp meetings were held there; I can just remember one in the yard in the open air. I think there would be fifty or sixty people there. My grandmother, Betsy Shirley of The Holmes played a mandolin. Her sister, Mary Jane, known as Ginny lived at Rewlach Farm. They were both Bassetts of Hulme End who had married two Shirley brothers. After special services, great aunt Ginny invited people back to the farm for a large meal.

One of my great grandfathers was John Wilshaw Bassett of West Side Mill, Hulme End. He had a lot to do with the Manifold Light Railway and was a farmer, builder, undertaker, corn merchant and had a coal business. He employed a lot of people. Mother used to say when he was holding an interview for anybody, he would leave a broom lying down outside the door and if the person picked it up, it would be a good indication for him to set them on. He built a lot of the good stone houses in the area.

My great aunt, Lizzie went to Reading University in the late 1800s to study dairying; possibly Professor Sheldon was instrumental in her going. This was unusual for a woman in those times. With her husband and children, she emigrated to Canada.

John Shirley in Homeguard outfit 1990s.

In the 1930s, during the miners' strike, times were very hard and they couldn't sell the cheese from the factory, so cheeses were stored in Longnor Town Hall and in the buildings at The Holmes. It was a very worrying time for my grandfather, Samuel Shirley, being the chairman of the Co-operative; the farmers were needing to be paid and they couldn't sell the cheese.

In the fields below Rewlach Chapel was Shirley Mill (Blakebrook, Blackbrook - old maps) where corn was ground; a barn remains there in which corn was stored. When the mill closed down, Grandfather took the stone and built a new building at The Holmes. Two millstones remain as door stones there too.

My brother-in-law went to South Africa recently and stayed with a friend. On a map of Johannesburg there was an area, Rewlatch, with a Shirley Street in the middle and his friend had gone to Rewlatch School. This is the only other mention of Rewlach that we've heard of.

EDWIN SHIRLEY (Claude)

Edwin Shirley lived at Oakenclough and he built a substantial stone bridge over the Oakenclough brook on the track to Newtown. There is a date stone E S 1871 on it. The story is related that he went into Longnor at the time of some election and got into a fight over politics. As a result of his injuries, he developed pneumonia and died in April 1871. The bridge was first used by the hearse carrying his body to the funeral.

Sheep at the Ridge.

Local lads' confirmation group at Warslow church in the early 1950s.

Believed to be at Hindlow station.

Ken Mellor

My grandfather, Jim Oliver went to work as a farm labourer for his aunt at Crow Trees between Warslow and Ecton. When he was 17, they were that short of fodder they had to go onto Ecton Hill and cut gorse and take it back and boil it up in the wash boiler to make it edible for the cattle.

He did a bit of poaching, he had a long coat with oilskin pockets in and used to go with a carbide lamp and a fork and get a few trout out of the Warslow brook, which he stored in the pockets. One night, he got back to the farm and 'Bobby' Frost was waiting for him. He said, *'I'll have what's i' th' left 'and pocket Jim, thee can keep what's int right!'*

He used to collect pee-wit eggs when they were in season and take 'em Leek Market to get a few coppers. It was legal to collect them, and curlew eggs, until 7th April. You generally took one out of each nest, unless there were four, when they may have started sitting. He used reckon to get up before daylight and go and wait till the sun was coming up and he could spot the eggs better. Of course, there were more about in those days; a man chain-harrowing with a horse could see the nests and avoid them and perhaps mark them.

He and his sister had had their voices trained for singing and he used to walk to the back of Ecton to the Pepper Inn to sing - so called because it was an unlicensed place for the lead and copper miners of the area to drink at and they used a peppercorn transaction instead of money.

When grandfather married, they eventually ended up at Monks Meadow Farm, near Chinley. The photo is Granny Lownds, his mother-in-law - there was no road down to the farm, so they put her onto an armchair in the milk or muck cart and took her down, then after tea took her back.

GORSE (Claude)

When our family was farming at Wormhill in the 1940s, we would use gorse for the base of our corn stacks. We fetched it from Wormhill Moor; it only grew in a quantity in one field near the pumping station. After it was cut, I remember using a hay fork to load it onto a trailer to take to wherever we were making a corn stack. We put it down in a circle about a foot thick rising to 2 feet in the middle and then built the corn sheaves onto it. When pressed down, it was a good tough layer which kept the bottom of the stack dry and was supposed to keep vermin out.

Longnor school children early 1960s.

Dowlow quarry

Peter Higton

I was born in 1923 at the paper shop in the market place at Longnor. Then we went to live down the cheese yard. Dad was an insurance agent for Prudential. He built Myrtle Cottages in 1933, well, he had them built; they cost £300. And Windy Ridge in 1935; that cost £500. He bought an old building for the stone, where old Sampy Riley had lived, near the Cheshire Cheese. Mr Bradbury, from Newtown, Walter Limer and Jess Hill did the work for him.

I left school at 14; I used to help doing farm work at Fold End; then went to Taylor's at Water Swallows, then to Shirley's at Rewlach . I was military age when war broke out, so I went for a medical and put in for RAF ground staff; but I was in a reserved occupation, so they didn't have me. There were two men working at Shirleys and Critchlows at Mosscar needed a man, so I went there. It was a good move; I had been getting £2 10s a week, but Critchlows paid me £5 a week, a lot of money then! It could be hurtful though when you were out on a Saturday night to be accused of *'hiding under cows tails'*. Though often the worst ones to say anything had never seen active service!

In 1955, I joined the Longnor Fire Service - Fire and Rescue now. I'd always been interested. You didn't have all the paraphernalia then, the medicals and stuff. The fire station was near the Crewe and Harpur then. Up the steps was HQ and office. The fire engine was outside in the garage. We met on a Thursday night, 7.30-9.30, checked the machine over to see if every thing was in order, then went upstairs. Sometimes, someone would come and give a lecture; you could be bored to tears sometimes; you could tell them more than they'd told you.

There were 8 or 9 of us; 6 would go on a call. The driver had to have a test and latterly we had breathing apparatus. I enjoyed it and I learnt first aid.

The first mill fire I went to was in Leek and we stopped all night. Two weeks later, there was another. Dennis Mellor was in charge and said to us, *'Now look, when you get there, whatever you do, look after yourselves; take no notice of what they tell you, don't go into the building unless you're in twos'.*

Harold Thompson, 'Little Alty', he worked on the Harpur Crewe estate. He could walk across the ridge of a house, no problem and go up a ladder like a cat. We had to go up a ladder and throw burnt stuff out. I said, *'Want me go up, Alty?'* *'They't o'rate colonel'.* He said. He used call me colonel. So I went up to the top, a full extender. When it came time to get down, I looked down and said, *'I daren't go down.'* He said, *'Don't take any notice, just step back and keep looking at me; walk down steady.'* The ladder was waving about. I got down but never did it again; it was a different 40ft than what we'd trained to.

One Good Friday, ten to midnight, the bell went and we turned out to a black and white heifer stuck in the fish pond at Ecton. We got there; we'd only got the searchlight on the machine. It had just got its head out and had been there for 12 hours; the people from the farm had been trying to get it out but couldn't do owt.

We carried two short lengths of hose for such purposes. We waded straight in, put them under and lifted it out bodily . It wanted some lifting, it had just about had enough; there were four of us, two on each side. There was a piece of rope in the cab; Alty made a halter and we got it down to the farm. It was very shaky. We put it in a building with some straw and rubbed it down. We got back to the station at about 3am. It was just another job to us. The RSPCA turned out after we left and we got a commendation. Longnor Fire Station Chief Officer was really chuffed.

A siren went off in the day and you had a bell in your house which rang at night. I worked at Mosscar; we had a lot of hay fires then and moor fires. In the daytime there were three of us on call; John Storer, the postman, was the officer in charge. One day the siren went and I came zooming down; Mrs Nadin on the corner used to wave me through. We turned out with three men. Hay fires were a terrible job; you had to get in a loft or building with smoke, stick it ten minutes, then come out for fresh air. It all had to be cleared out smouldering, even if it took a week. There was supposed to be a fresh crew sent in after so many hours, but they didn't always arrive.

We were glad of the money, it was very handy. When I joined, it was £1 for turnout and 25 bob an hour while you were out. Response time was 7 minutes, from work to get on the machine and away. Norman Coates from Barrow Moor was furthest away then. Before I finished, we had an alerter which you fitted on your belt and had to charge up every night.

One dry summer around 1960, on a Sunday morning, I'd just come from work when John Storer rang. 'How are you fixed today if we get any callouts?' I said 'Alright.' No sooner had I said that when the siren kicked in. There were only three of us, me, John and Trevor Grimshaw, all the others were on holiday. The call was to Newtown; someone had set some gorse on fire, but by the time we got there it had more or less gone out. We got back and booked 'available' - Longnor 1 was our callout then. We had to turnout on standby Longton way. We'd never been much further than Leek and hadn't a clue where to go. We zoomed into Leek fire station, but there was not a soul about, everybody had gone. We carried on and saw a police car, so asked them for directions. It was 1.30 by now; there had been a fire that morning at a big hotel, grass over peat which had ignited again. The hydrant was 200yds down the road. We stopped 2hrs and really soaked it. All the time on the radio they were asking, 'Hello Longnor, have you finished there, are you available?' So we booked 'available.' There was a housing estate where during the war they had built tanks to store water and they had since got filled with rubbish which someone had ignited and they were close to the back of houses. They'd had garden hoses and stopped it getting to the houses. We hadn't had a drink of tea or a bite of anything. We got there and they came out with plates of corned beef sandwiches and a gallon jug of tea.

We stopped there till 7 at night; we had to keep lugging the hoses round. Kids came; they were black helping out, but they enjoyed it. We booked available and another job came in, a fire somewhere else in Staffordshire, a fair way off. It was 9 when we got there. We were on top of a hill and down in the bottom was a river with gorse bushes and trees. It was just like the illuminations going like the clappers. We'd had enough. A bloke came up to us, the first officer we'd seen all day, he said, *'Where's your officer?' 'In the cab.'* I said. *'Right, I want 2 of your men to do this and 2 to do that and 2 more to...'* John Storer says, 'Hang on mate, *there's only three of us.' 'What! You've turned out with 3 men?' 'Yes and we're ready for home.'* So he let us go. It was half past 1 in the morning when we finished.

Out on a moor fire, you could be there all night mauling hoses about. It was a big job; they were in 20ft lengths, wet through and covered in peat and mud. Then you'd bring them back and scrub them and hang them to dry in the drying tower and replace with fresh hoses ready to turn out again. When you came back from a fire, you hadn't finished, there was another hour's work tidying up. The hoses were made of heavy canvas; they are much easier to handle nowadays.

Peter receiving his long service medal in 1976.
L-R: Ken Thompson, Bob Smith, - -, Trevor Grimshaw, - -, Bob Clarke, Peter, John Storer, Ken Stevens.

Peter in his Hollinsclough bandsman's uniform.

A good pump man would have the water on before you'd got your hose out and nozzle on ready for action. Once a station officer from Stafford came out to try and tell us how to do it, how it had to be done, but he didn't get a very good reception!

There was a haystack fire on Fairfield Common and we turned out to it on *'assistance call'*. Buxton fire service was there but all they did was squirt every time they saw a flame. Norman Coates was with us; we had two cutting knives; me and Bob Smith set to cutting round this stack, Norman sharpening. We cut 18 inches off all round the stack and saved it. Th' owd lad came up with a basket of beer for us and rollocked Buxton for 'playing around.' We got the credit, but it was just another job.

If the bell went off at night, while I was getting my trousers on, my wife was in the bathroom rinsing my false teeth. Then she'd stand by the front door with it wide open ready and teeth in her outstretched hand and I put them in running down the street. I liked to smoke a pipe after a job and it were no use without teeth . I used run down in my slippers and lose them, so I ran in my stocking feet.

I played in Hollinsclough band; they practised at Mosscar. I started playing the double bass, then when they couldn't get a drummer, I took that job. We did Flash Club Feast for years; it was alright when the weather was nice. When it was hot it used to melt the tar on the road. We set off and played out of the village, then knocked off till we were within 50yds of the Travellers Rest. But I had to keep playing to keep the beat going to keep in step, but your feet used to stick so it was hard to keep right and if it was windy, it caught the drum.

At Folly Rest camp meeting we played hymns, then knocked off and went into a long kitchen in the farmhouse. There was a table down the middle where the band sat. It was a good spread. There was always a big plate of ham sandwiches and one of the band members always sat against it; he never talked, just looked after them sandwiches! He played the euphonium. He always enjoyed his tea at Folly Rest. Afterwards, we played a few marches, then at 6 o'clock struck in and played for the night service.

I was in the homeguard and when it disbanded in 1947, Colonel Worthington was taking the salute in Longnor Square. There were 200 homeguard in the area; it was a big final parade. We set off from the market place, marched round and came back onto the front of the Crewe and Harpur to be disbanded. I hadn't been drumming long in them days; I'd got this drumstick and bit of string round my wrist. Coming down past the post office, the string broke and the stick dropped about a yard in front of me. I picked it up and came in dead on the beat again, I only missed one beat. We played the national anthem and that were it. I says to John Thomas Grindey, the conductor after, *'I had a bit of a do up road.' 'I 'eard it lad.'* He knew. If I hadn't have come in dead on the beat, it would have been chaos in front of a lot of people. I had a leather strap after that.

In wartime a bloke came to Mosscar one day. We'd just killed a pig; it were hung up. *'Ow much for th' 'am lad?'* He asked Charles. *'It's not for sale.' 'I'll give you £90.'* He says, which in them days was terrific. *'It's not for sale, I've got some good men working for me (one were me); when they've done a good day's work same as at haytime, they have a good feed.' 'That's too good to give men.'* Charles flew at him and said, *'Hang on; There's men and men!'*

After 45 yrs at Mosscar, I got a long service certificate. I went to Stoneleigh to be presented with it by the Duke of Gloucester. I'm 84 now, I'd do it all over again, I've enjoyed my work.

ALSTONFIELD DEANERY MAGAZINE.

THE ANNUAL SUNDAY SCHOOL PRIZE GIVINGS.

These were held on the first and second Sundays after Easter. Through the great kindness of Lady Crewe, the Vicar was enabled to provide and give, with Miss Limer's and Miss Shaw's assistance, a number of Prayer and Hymn Books and other gift books at Longnor, Newtown, and Reapsmoor, on each occasion giving a suitable address.

Those who received prizes at Longnor received them for behaviour as well as for over half attendances. They were Hilda Bradbury, Dolly Caley, Connie Caley, Tom Nadin, Frank Caley, Alice A. Grindey, Annie Bradbury, Willie Gilman, Gladys Robinson, Sam Weston, J. T. Grindey, Ed. Preston, Geo. Preston, Fred Gilman, Jack Percival, Chas. Weston, Grace Robinson, Chas. Percival, Mary Johnson, E. Gilman.

REAPSMOOR ROOL OF HONOUR.

Pte. Victor Kidd—Northumberland Fusiliers.
Sapper Chas. Cope—R.E.
Gunner Jessie Wood—R.G. Artillery.
Gunner John Prince—R.F.A.
Pte. Jas. Edge—N. Staffs.

We are thankful to say these are all well, and are serving their country manfully. Some have been out since the beginning of the War.

We grieve to think of the loss the Vicar of Alstonfield has sustained by the death in action of his son, Lieut. E. Brown, whose early years were spent at Longnor. Reapsmoor has sustained one loss in Pte. Fred Kirkham; Longnor in Pte. Jn. Bowman, and our sympathy has gone out towards those who were related.

NEWTOWN.

The following letter has been received from Lieut.-General Congreve:

April 26.

Dear Miss Lymer,

Your parcel of socks arrived to-day and very grateful I am for them and send my thanks on behalf of my men to you and your scholars for their kindness in thinking of us in so practical a way. I send the socks down to our baths, where the men are given clean clothing, each time they come. We get through enormous quantities and always have a demand for all we can supply despite the excellent way in which the Ordnance meet our demands.

All goes well out here, everyone is confident and cheerful, and I am sure you all are the same at home.—Believe me, very truly yours,

WM. CONGREVE, Lieut.-Gen.

Headquarters, 13th Corps.

I have never been wounded I am glad to say. I wonder how the report got to you.

Cuttings from the Alstonefield Deanery Magazine. Above, June 1916, on the right, April 1909.

Mr Lomas, local preacher, with Josie and Ben Mellor.

Quarnford and Ramshaw.

The very heavy snow which still lies banked up in our roads has interrupted many branches of work. It has also to some extent interfered with our church services. On March 7th both roads from the Vicarage to Ramshaw were quite snowed up. The Vicar, after reconnoitring on horseback on both roads, had to abandon the Ramshaw service. It was just as well he did not struggle through, as he was not expected, and no fires were lighted in the schoolroom. In the morning it was thought that no service could be held in the parish church, nevertheless both services were held. In the afternoon some 18 persons managed to brave the snowdrifts, and in the evening 22.

There has not been as much snow on the road between Quarnford and Leek for many years, certainly not for the last 10 years. Fortunately no arrangement was made for special preachers for Lent, as they would have found it difficult to come and go. The Vicar has had to refuse invitations elsewhere for that reason.

EMIGRATION.

Just before winter three of our young men, Joseph and Harold Townson, from the Schoolhouse, and Herbert Heathcote, from Brandside, went to Australia. Good news has been heard of them, and we wish them health and prosperity in their new home. Now two more of our young men are going to Canada, viz., John Mellor, of Drystone Edge, and Samuel Goodwin, of Knotbury. The former has been in Canada before, and is going back to the firm he has worked for out there, but S. Goodwin is going out for the first time, with Mr. Oliver, of Gradbach, who went out some 20 years ago, and has done very well there. S. Goodwin was given a Bible by the Vicar, and some of the members of the Reading-room, as a parting gift and an expression of good wishes. We are also pleased to hear a good account of the son and two daughters of Mr. N. Kidd, who are now in Canada.

A lecture on Canada will be given in the schoolroom on May 1st.

We are glad to think that all these young people are still under the British flag. May they also continue under the banner of the Cross.

1950s. Longnor Carnival Queen.

Longnor NFU December 1954.

Choir at Longnor 1930s. Emma Mellor, organist, far right.

Longnor School, 1940s.

Frank Bagnall

Grandad kept the farm and mill at Glutton. He was supposed be black sheep of family, but 'e must 'ave bought the farm cuz 'e owned it. He ground corn, milked cows and kept a lot o' pigs. When I remember it, they 'adn't got many sows but they 'ad boars which people bought their sows to. The last boar was a big large white and they 'ad wale 'im. I remember seein' red lines down 'is back. Some woman used come from Longnor with a pig t'th' boar; walk it down. It were cowd weather an me granfather said t'th' woman, 'Yo'd better go inside missus an' 'ave a cup o'tea, these lads'll do th' boar for yer.' *'I'm non doin that!'* 'er sez, *'I did that last time an' I'd neow bloody pigs!'* I think 'er name were Thora.

The Bagnall family at Glutton, Golden Wedding 1921. IN FRONT Nelly.
BACK: Dolly, Jack, Phoebe, Grandad George, Elsie, Mary Jane, George, Marion.
FRONT: Tommy, Ida, Dad Joe, Granny Mary, Fanny, Sal.

I can only remember corn comin' down chutes an' water bashin' on t'th' wheel turnin'. He'd only grind a bit then. They used let dam off every once in a while ter clear t' sand out o't' channel an' get no end o' fish an' sell 'em in Buxton - wind gate up, let it off an' get silt off bottom. Trout! Supposed be th' finest trout thee is in th' country. I've picked 'em out fer folks as are dyin', owd stagers from round 'ere. They just fancied a trout.

When the were all this corn about, they kept the rats down wi' cats. They went Leek one Wednesday an' brought two cats back from some pub. When they went agen, th' next Wednesday, they'd gone back agen.

No cars in them days, they kept trotters; they wanted take some of 'is 'orses in t' first war. I remember Poppy at Abbotside, that trotter o' Joe Bagshaw's. Stuck its front feet right out; I remember seein' 'em go past once. Th'owd woman looked that little agen 'im, but 'e'd got one o' them tall velvet 'ats on. They reckon that Poppy could come from t' Cheese in Buxton to Abbotside in 18 minutes. It were '32 when it died; buried somewhere at Abbotside. Ee it could go!

Dad came up 'ere to Underhill in '22, his mother and sister were at mill when owd feller died. I were born in '24. When I was 13, I started work for Charlie Slack at Home Farm, Earl Sterndale. You were put to work in them days. 'E'd come 'ere an' seen me milkin' an' got round our owd feller ter let may goo with 'im from summer 'olidays till Easter. Dad were fit then. They were o'rate wi' me; I stopped fer two an' 'alf year an' go school as well; lived in wi' 'em. Very nice woman, Lizzie, they'd no family. I 'ad clean cows out before I went school. Harry Chappell 'ud be goin past, goin; t' Hillhead quarry; an' Jack Mycock an' Jack Riley comin' up with 'is father an' goin' past. That school teacher then, Miss Price used live at Glutton an' used get canned up. 'Er'd be still tiddly on Monday.

Next, I did a year with Jane Riley at Pilsbury Top. Then inter th' quarries. Doing 12 an' 'alf 'ours a day when they bombed church. Thinkin' I were doin' summat, just a lad, I went Dowlow. I did anythin'. Wouldn't let me go fillin' up, werena quite old enough the foreman said. So what did they bloody do? Put me ont' that job, what they call a powder monkey. 'Uggin bloody gel, saxonite, amynil, fuses, caps an' gunpowder. I were goin' t' top lift, lenchin, gas kilns, bottom lift, carryin' it; an' a bloody lad shouldn't 'a bin among that, I found out after.

That owd feller, they said 'e were mad; 'e 'ad brown whiskers with a hole through where 'is fag 'ad burned. I were goin' up ter this magazine, a piece off. When y' went in, yer were supposed slip into these big shoes, stop any sparks, an' y'ad a brass 'ammer. Gunpowder were in back an' I thowt, *'Bloody 'ell, doors cummin' to on me.'* It were that owd mon; 'e must 'a bin 'idin' t' see if I'd got them shoes on; which I 'ad. Brass 'ammer were t' open boxes o' gunpowder so yer didn't make a spark. It 'ad brass nails an' y'ad a brass chisel. Then y'ad get white bag o' gunpowder out an' lug it t' top lift or anywhere.

While I were in th' quarries, I were in th' 'omeguard. I went regular t' Earl Sterndale trainin', slopin' arms, shootin', owe sorts. 30 or more of us on some concrete by th' Quiet Woman. We did

Territorial Army camps between Hindlow and Harpur Hill around 1930. Taken by Jim Finney.

exercises anywhere an' shootin' in th' quarry. I'd never used one o' them rifles before; I only got two on the top corner o'th' target, I missed with three. Tommy and Stan Milner were th' best shots. Then they looked at mine and said, 'If 'e can hit that, 'e can kill a man. So they wanted me be a sniper.

Joe Sweetmore were picked out be a despatch rider, cus 'e'd got a motorbike. One o' them buggers with pips on used come in a Morris 8, black an' green from near Buxton. He set about Joe cause 'e 'adn't turned up. I think 'e'd bin Meerbrook way after some woman; said 'e'd 'ad stop with a cow. It went quiet, then somebody shouted from th' back, 'Ow many legs 'ad 'er, Joe!' I always remember that.

Anyway a doctor or some professional out o' Buxton 'ad come down Long 'Ill from Manchester an' reckoned 'e'd seen summat come down. They came round 'ere and searched 'ouses; they thowt somebody 'ad dropped. Last I 'eard, it was supposed be a barrage balloon broke loose from Manchester. Be about 1942.

If your national insurance number ended in 1 or 9 you were balloted t' go down th' mines, so I were nabbed, a Bevin boy. In the war y'ad t' go, but where were the sense in me trainin' t' be a sniper, then be sent down the pit! That were September 44 to February 46.

I 'ad various jobs; it could be $3^{1}/_{2}$ miles under from where yer go down. Two owd men were pullin' all th' props out; scrawlin' about in a 2 foot 6 deep passage. I was pullin' 'em back on me 'ands an' knees with kneepads on t' where they could be loaded up when this roof came in. Lamp were no good, couldna see nowt fer a bit.

Th' worst job was to watch th' main conveyer, where two more were comin' in from th' sides, tippin' on. You 'a't watch it an' stop it if there was a problem. When y'd 'ad 8 hours o' that, ye'r black an' can't get it out o' yer eyes; y've a job see. The most borin' job, but the money were there, £5 a week. In the quarry, it were about 28s a week in wartime, but I thowt anythin's better than 5 am t' midnight farmin' then.

I biked from 'ere to Bolsover and lodged with a woman; 'er 'usband lay in bed wantin' a drink.

When I come in, 'e shouted for me; 'is 'ead were covered in sweat, 'e'd got terrible pain and d'yer know where it was? In the leg 'e 'adn't got; 'e'd lost a leg in th' mine. When I first got there, I opened a door by mistake and there were three pink legs with no body on 'em; give may a shock, that did, in like a cupboard.

They tried nab me for conscription after but Dad 'ad took bad wi' 'is chest, wi' bein' in t' mill; th' dust 'ad done 'im. So I 'ad come 'ome; doctor recommended it.

There were an owd mon lived on Hollinsclough Moor; 'e were in bed 18 year an' 'e smoked in bed. There were 'oles everywhere, I think 'e set th' piller on fire, all roads. 'E'd five pipes, they filled 'em for 'im. An' 'ow old d'yer think 'e was when 'e died? 100 years an' ten months.

WHY LONGNOR? (Claude)

Ancient ridge and furrow system.

The name Longnor is derived from the Anglo-Saxon Longenovre, meaning on the long flat-topped ridge with the convex shoulder. Unlike Longnor in Shropshire, which has developed from Langanalre (place at the tall alder tree) or Longenolre (long alder copse).

The ridge starts above the River Dove at Nab End and runs from there in a south-east direction with the village sitting in the middle facing south, 250 yards from the River Manifold; the ridge forming a natural barrier between the two river valleys. The village was on an important cross roads with plenty of good spring water and good all round visibility.

It was once a more important place commercially than Buxton, which was recorded in 1781 as a hamlet before its growth in the Georgian period. Longnor has always had many inns - licenses were granted in 1604 to 8 men to keep alehouses and in an 1818 directory, 7 inns are listed.

In the early 1800s, there was a candle factory, two bakeries, several grocers and a growing number of shoemakers - 8 in 1851. There were butchers, masons, joiners, drapers, two blacksmiths, two saddlers, two wheelwrights, two tailors, two auctioneers, a surgeon, a miller, a gentleman's outfitter, a registrar, a druggist, watchmaker etc. (J Nichol, *St Bartholomew's. Church and Parish*)

I know of no defensive engineering, but earthworks, possibly fortifications can be seen from above Crowdicote looking across towards Knowsley Hill. When the light is right and

shadows are cast, they look impressive. There are signs of intensive farming work, ridge and furrow, on what was the Town field and an area known as Longnor Wharf was a place where packhorse trains met and loads were exchanged.

Just beyond Longnor Bridge by the Manifold is Longnor Mill. There was a mill recorded near here in 1404, known as Frith Mill In 1605, Sir John Harpur replaced it and it was later rebuilt by a corn dealer and chapman, Richard Gould of Warslow. In 1831 it was a corn mill and included a bone mill, and in the late 1800s it was a saw mill and rakes were made there. (*Victoria County History*)

In 1932 there was a fire at Longnor Mill. The Harpur-Crewe estate used the premises as their estate yard, cutting up trees and doing carpentry and joinery work using the water wheel to power the machinery. There was also a blacksmith's shop. The fire left the premises a gutted shell; the top storey was unsafe and had to be taken down and the roof replaced. Then they carried on until about thirty years ago.

Mr Sykes in his workshop

William Billinge, buried in Longnor churchyard.
He was born under a hedge in a cornfield in 1679
He was severely wounded as a soldier, and a musket ball
lodged in his thigh for 30 years until it worked its way
out.. He carefully preserved it until his death.

In Memory of William Billinge, who was born in a Cornfield, at Fawfieldhead, in this Parish, in the Year 1679. At the age of 23 years he enlisted into His Majesty's Service under Sir George Rooke, and was at the taking of the Fortress of Gibraltar, in 1704. He afterwards served under the Duke of Marlborough at the ever Memorable Battle of Ramillies, fought on the 23rd of May, 1706, where he was wounded by a musket shot in the thigh. He afterwards returned to his native country, and with manly courage defended his Sovereign's rights at the Rebellion in 1715 and 1745. He died within the space of 150 yards of where he was born, and was interred here the 30th of January, 1791, aged 112 years.
Billited by Death, I quartered here remain,
When the trumpet sounds, I'll rise and march again.

Longnor Players 1920s. The Mikado.

LOT 157.

(Coloured Red on Plan No. 4).

"THE MERMAID INN"

Area : 154 Acres, 2 Roods, 19 Perches.

Tenant : J. Ward.

Tenancy : Yearly, 25th March.

Rent : £44.

A Country Inn (Six-Day Licence) and Land

Situate in the Parish of Onecote adjoining a main road.

The Inn is constructed of stone with a tiled roof and contains: Entrance Passage, Tap Room, with Small Bar, Parlour, Kitchen, Pantry. Cellar, Three Bedrooms and Boxroom, E.C., and Coalplace.

The Farmbuildings comprise : Stable, Cowshed for 5, Cowshed for 10, two pig styes, Stirk Shed for 2.

The Land lies in three blocks with frontages to three main roads.

SCHEDULE

Staffs. iv. 15 and 16 (1925).

O.S. No.		Description.	Area.
1	...	Moor	1.813
1a	...	Ditto	.057
2	...	Ditto	144.686
6	...	Grass	2.929
7	...	Ditto	2.464
8	...	Inn and Buildings	.377
11	...	Grass	2.292
			154.618

Land Tax 11s. 10d. per annum, payable by Tenant.

There is reserved out of this Lot a Right of Way for the owner of Lot 155 over the Bridle Road in O.S. No. 2, forming part of this Lot.

LOT 202.

(Coloured Blue on Plan No. 4).

"SHINING FORD"

Area : 10 Acres, 1 Rood, 2 Perches.

Tenant : J. Bradbury.

Tenancy : Yearly, 25th March.

Rent : £15 5s. 0d. (Apportioned).

A Smallholding and Smithy

Situate in the Parishes of Heathylee and Fawfieldhead.

The House, constructed of stone with a tiled roof contains : Living Room, Kitchen, Pantry, Cellar, Two Bedrooms, E.C. and Coalplace.

The Buildings, constructed of stone with tiled roofs, comprise : Store Shed with loft over, Cowshed for 7, Mixing Place with loft over, Blacksmith's Shop and Forge with store shed over.

The Land lies in a ring fence and is watered by the Oakenclough Brook.

SCHEDULE

Staffs. v. 5 (1922).

O.S. No.		Description.	Area.
15	...	Grass	.090
43	...	Ditto	.878
44	...	Ditto	1.276
45	...	Ditto	1.646
46	...	House, Buildings and Grass ...	1.299
47	...	Grass	.954
517	...	Ditto	2.598
518	...	Ditto	1.292
534	...	Ditto	.228
			10.261

Young Longnor about 1890.

1890 Longnor School.

Cheadle Road.

Leek Road and Gauledge.

John Critchlow and John Worthington.

Dad and Henry Armitt 1960s.

Hilda Critchlow

There are four of us, my sister Frances was born at Boothlow in 1919. I came along in 1928 and I've heard it said me Dad wanted a boy and he cried when I was born, but I've done my share since. I was the first child born here for 100 years. Then there's my brothers, George and John.

This place has only been called Sheldon House since George went to Cubley in 1960. It was all called The Brund; next door was New House, then my cousin Gilbert came to Small Brund the other side, so that was Critchlows at Brund as well, so to avoid confusion they called it Lime Tree Farm. Of course this had no name then and the solicitor knew John Prince Sheldon had lived here, so he called it Sheldon Farm.

Thomas Johnson and Henry used to call on a Sunday morning and they said, *'Don't call it Sheldon Farm, call it Sheldon House'*. And that's how the places are now distinguished.

When J P Sheldon was here, the buildings were all up where the garden is now and the story goes that Mrs Sheldon had

Hilda and John Critchlow.

got some money and they wanted to put water into Sheen village. It didn't happen, so they spent the money putting the buildings down the yard here. There are two stones, one with J P S and the other M E S, that's Margaret Ellen Sheldon. The date is 1888. He was a professor of agriculture and went abroad studying. They died in 1913 and 1914 and the farm was sold; it made £4,000. Our grandfather bought it just because this Sheldon, a noted man in those days, had lived here. Folks around said, *'Old Critchlow has gone mad!'* Our family has added land to it since.

Sheldon House.

Dad, James, worked at home at Pump Farm, Warslow. Mother was a Grindon from next door and because they were having to get married - my sister was on the way - the Grindons offered her a little cottage down the yard. Dad thought he'd never get a farm; he'd have to

Henry, George, John, Mum and Dad in the hayfield 1950s.

Dad and John, and Colin Beresford.

Warslow Band 1917.

keep working at home. Uncle George lived at Boothlow and offered for her to go there and aunty looked after her. Then this place became vacant and they came here in 1920.

Grandfather died in1941 and left half of the farm to Uncle George and half to Dad. So Uncle George said he would either buy or sell the other half, so Dad bought the half off him and Uncle George bought Low End Farm and went there.

We rent a piece of land known as Sep's Ground from what were known as Onecote Poor People. This Sep was up at Top Boothlow and he rented it previously. He died in 1927 and we took it from 1928. The rent used to be £8 and we always paid the money to the vicar.

I remember we built stacks of corn in this little field near the farm and held off thatching, waiting for Belfields contractors to come with their thrashin' drum. It was about like waitin' for the shearer to come. Of course, they hadn't time to come yet, so Dad would thatch the stacks and then within a day or two they decided to come threshin'. I can remember goin' up onto the moors with Dad, mowin' the rushes for thatchin' and then handin' him the thatch up and the thatch pegs, which he made himself out of hazel.

John hacked out this little field with the scythe up until two years ago; that is cutting the edges out; Dad used to do every field, he always took a pride in it. In one field, where the muck was thrown from the barn in winter, there always grew a lot of docks. They used to mow them and send me to collect them up, saying, *'We'll come to yer.'* But they never did and I had to do it meself, it was a hateful job.

We grew cabbages; at planting, I used to hold them and Dad had a spade and dug in, then I had to put the cabbage plant in, and as he pulled the spade out he used catch my hand. I always wore high-topped shoes, not Wellingtons and soil used go in them. And also holding the two horses, one was a grey one and went harder than the brown one and I had to pull it back and it was kicking soil in my boots and I could do nothing about it. Nowadays you'd just chelp and say you couldn't do it, you daresn't then. I was about 15 then and outside all the time; hand-milking 'til I was 21. We had about 30 cows.

We used keep about 100 pigs; Dad and John went round local farms buyin' weaners. We fattened them on meal and whey which we fetched from Hartington cheese factory twice a week in a tank. It cost 5d a gallon, that was in the 60s. We sold them into Sheffield to be killed, to McCrackens. Arch Belfield took them for us, he had a wagon.

We kept a lot of hens, 400 or more at times. Mr Woolley from Rushton picked the eggs up. We made cheese in wartime; we borrowed a cheese kettle from Mrs Salt. And we took a drop of cream off the milk every morning to make our own butter. Mother made oat cakes; she put the stuff in a milk bucket in a morning and let it stand, then cooked them after dinner.

Our milk went to Sheffield and Eccleshall Co-op; it was moved by Shimwells of Youlgreave. It only went to Hartington for a short while, when we went onto the bulk tank. I've heard Dad say it used to go to Express at Rowsley and somebody came here from Wiggenstall after the contract; it was a penny a gallon more money if Dad could get so many to sign with him. I was 13 then and I was sent round neighbours with these contracts.

A bit of post would come on a Friday - I called him Friday postman to his face . Now there's never a day but they don't drop somethin' off, either a bill or some mither. But I'm still goin', still helpin' milkin' at 79. I think I must be mad when I see people walking past in their free time, but I've enjoyed it.

Harry Gee

I was born at The Hayes, Reapsmoor in 1923 and Christened William Henry, but most people know me as Harry. Dad was Arthur Gee and Mum was Amy Riley from Higg Lane End. They were at The Hayes for 9 years; we left in 1927 and came here to Ridge Farm. Both farms were owned by the Harpur-Crewe estate, practically all these farms were at that time, 'til they 'ad that big sale in 1951, when we bought this.

Dad's family were at New Road, where they 'ad a corn business, groceries shop and petrol pump; grandfather Isaac Gee 'ad started it up and when 'e died quite young, grandma Gee and their sons carried it on. There were seven lads, Sampson, who went to Fleet Green, Jim, who went to Manchester into the police force, Isaac, Robert, Dad, Henry and William, and a girl who died when she was 7.

Uncle Bob trained for a joiner at Hulme End, they used call it the Woodshop, opposite the turning for Sheen. Then 'e ran 'is business from New Road in a shed at this end o'th 'ouse. 'E did all sorts, farm joinery, carts, gates, anythin', all 'and tools then, no machines.

Harry

The corn business carried on 'til late 30s, then fizzled out; I would think the big corn firms were sendin' travellers round and there were two corn stores in Longnor, Charlie Batkin's and Tom Belfield's.

When I was going to school, Charlie Batkin's place was on the back street, just past the church, it's a house now. He was unloadin' some straw and whether they were pullin' some out from the bottom, but 'e over-balanced off the wagon, fell onto the road, hit 'is 'ead and died from 'is injuries.

Tom Belfield was where Masseys are now and he sold out to Loose & Co, always known as Loose's to most people.

At New Road, they 'ad a carriers cart, a cart with seats on each side and people locally as 'ud come int' th' shop an' corn store 'ud ask if they could go Leek with yer on Wednesday and Dad took it every Wednesday; that were 'is job. They used the biggest strongest horse and when they were comin' back agen, if they'd a fair lot o' shoppin' on, when they got t' th' bottom o' Thorncliffe Bank, two or three on 'em 'ud 'ave get out an' walk up. It were too much fer one horse take 5 or 6 people up an' a fair bit o' shoppin' as well.

When me Dad left school, 'e went t' Professor Sheldon at Brund; 'e were th' horseman there. 'E used go out in summer travellin' with an entire - Kingston Minestral - to people's mares. 'E'd go out on a Monday mornin' and come back Friday teatime, stayin' out overnight. 'E never drove a tractor or motor or anythin', just horses. Dad lived there at The Brund until they died. The Light Railway was goin' then and Mrs Sheldon 'ud appen be goin' Leek or further on somewhere. She'd 'ave be taken down t' Hulme End an' get on th' train an' 'e'd 'ave meet 'er back; everythin' went to time.

THORS CAVE, MANIFOLD VALLEY.
NORTH STAFFORDSHIRE RAILWAY.

THE LIGHT RAILWAY

'E 'ad £12 a year, paid once, at Christmas an' 'e always 'ad t' buy a new suit, because 'e did all the drivin'. There used t' be Beswick's Lime Works at Hindlow an' the Sheldons were very friendly with them an' 'e had to drive them there; they 'ad plenty of horses.

Professor Sheldon used write for a magazine and 'e went to America quite a bit; 'e'd go a time or two a year and 'e'd buy quite a bit of agricultural machinery - 'e were a bit of a pioneer. 'E bought Deering horse mowers, quite a few, they'd come over 'ere an' 'e'd sell 'em on agen. We 'ad a Deering two-horse mower, it 'ad a wider cutter bar and you could get on better.

Of course I started with horses and a lot of hand work as well. I enjoyed it, but when tractors came in, that was the way things were goin' and you went along with it. We used take the horses to Bill Mellor at Higg Lane fer shoein'. 'E was a good blacksmith an' fast.

Uncle Arthur Riley lived at Crowdicote, 'e was a blacksmith in the quarry doin' metalwork. The stone wagons that they filled by hand always wanted some repair work doin'. Jack was 'is son, 'e trained at Higg Lane with Bill Mellor. All the Rileys were tradesmen, mother's dad were joiner and undertaker at Higg Lane End. There were 5 little cottages there and Robert Riley, mother's grandfather had 5 children and 'e bought all 5 cottages for 85 guineas out of 'is waistcoat pocket and gave 'em one each.

There was a school at Reapsmoor, where children generally went until they were 9, then into Longnor; but I started Longnor when I was 5; walked the mile and a half each way. I 'ad three older sisters, Margaret, Amy and Doris, I went with them and there were Shirleys girls, Vera, Enid and Lola at The Holmes, Jack Higton, Sam Wood, one or two off Reapsmoor, Joyce from Broadham, John Sutton and Betty, two Rileys from across the road 'ere, 11 from School Clough. When they were all on the road, there were between 20 and 30 if you all met up at the same time.

Shirley's girls used call 'ere an' when we werena quite ready, they'd wait an' we'd all set off t'gether. Jack Higton an' Phyllis, Dennis an' them, used walk from Rewlach; a long walk in all weathers, yer could be wet through when yer got school.

There used come a milk wagon up past 'ere with churns on an' sometimes I used get a lift with 'im. 'E'd lift me on t' th' wagon; I stood between the churns and 'e'd get out at Longnor an' lift me off agen . If yer did that t'day, they'd lock yer up.

Then there were kids from Brownspit an' Critchlows at Boothlow. When they were all at Longnor School, Mr Bolton, the headmaster used put it up on a blackboard every day how many there were there. There'd be 138 or140.

I was bullied at times on the way to school by a big lad from a neighbouring farm, but Sam Wood, 'e was a good friend, 'e used come to the rescue . I reckon I was odd one out, only being 5 an' the others goin' t' Reapsmoor 'til they were 9.

On the way t'school, we'd meet Joel Carrington comin' this way on 'is motorbike with 'is sister, Mona on pillion. She was a teacher at Reapsmoor school, a young lass then. They lived at Tunstead at top o' Longnor. One mornin' goin' round the corner at Park House, they came off; perhaps goin' too fast on loose gravel and she badly hurt her leg and was off work quite a while; she learnt drive later an' 'ad an Austin 7.

Jim Cundy was local butcher. Opposite the school is the road past the church and the lane goin' up is Lane Head; we always called it Cundy lane. At the bottom end, there's double doors an' that was butchers shop. 'Is buildings were a few yards up the lane where 'e killed 'is beasts. When we were goin' school, 'e used get some o' the big strong lads to 'old on t'th' rope which went through a ring in the floor to 'old the beast while 'e killed it.

Mr Nesbitt kept the Post-Office an' Miss Knowles 'ad a little shop on the end; her front door an' front room is where the shop is now. She was a spinster; she sold a bit of most things, sweets, groceries and at Christmas time, stuff for kids, toys an' little Christmas stockins.

Bill Turner from Cuckoo Stones at the Ridge 1930s.

Uncle Will 'ad a new wagon, a four wheeler and when they weren't makin' cheese at the factory, he'd take the churns of milk from Reapsmoor to Rowsley, where it was put on the train.

My wife was June Grindey; her family came from Ilam t' Badgers Croft and she went school at Newtown. Ruth Hand was head teacher there. Once, one o' the girls from Fleetgreen broke her ankle an' June an' three or four o' these big girls 'ad t' carry her home t' Fleetgreen on a chair; Miss Hand sent 'em.

Cousin Sampson Gee jnr at Fleetgreen was buyin' Standard Fordsons an' sellin' 'em on agen. We 'ad first one off 'im second 'and about 1948. In 1963, we 'ad a new Fordson Dexter out of Bassetts Garage at Hartington; where that craft shop is now, near the water fountain. Bassetts was taken over by a Halifax firm in the 1940s and they brought this tractor down from Halifax an' stood it in th' showroom for quite a bit. That was at the front and further back was the workshop with petrol pumps on the front. They'd 'ad it long enough, all it 'ad done was move a few vehicles about in th' yard at Halifax; it 'ad 6 or 7 hours on the clock. It cost £465, we've still got it.

As for the Harper-Crewes, some of it was alright, some werena so good. When we first came 'ere, a chap named Pemberton were th' agent; 'e lived at Alstonefield. If you wanted somethin' doin', Dad 'ud get Pemberton 'ere

Johnny Grindey and Herbert Lomas working at the Ridge for the Harper-Crewe estate 1930s.

an' ask if they'd do it. Oh ah, 'e'd agree to it; then nowt 'appened an' when y' got onto 'im agen, 'e'd gone off th' idea; suppose it was the money. This place was 97 acres and the rent was £110.

They'd quite a few men at Longnor Mill, stonemasons, joiners and the like. Course, the rumour locally was that's 'ow they came by some o' these properties. They'd offer ter do some repairs for other people if they were slack, an' then if they couldn't afford to pay, eventually the Harpur-Crewes got the farm.

They were one of the biggest landowners in the country at one time; bit eccentric some on 'em. One o' the descendants once told me there were two brothers who didn't get on. One went abroad - maybe in the army an' 'e was gone some time. And while 'e was gone, the other razed 'is 'ouse t'th' ground an' soiled it over; they 'ated one another that much.

Miss Airmyne, from Warslow Hall left quite a bit o' money to Newtown Church; she seemed quite connected and supported them a lot. Harpur-Crewes used pay the teacher's wages at Reapsmoor School . I'm goin' back a bit, before the council took it over. Mr Shirley at Rewlach used to pay the teachers on their behalf. They also used pay the curate for Newtown and Reapsmoor churches.

When Grandma Gee was at The Low, there were 5 families living there; two families of Goulds, Gilmans, Edges and Wheeldons. All the land was split up, it wasn't like it is now. Down the road, there's a field at the back o' Park House and a barn in it known as Wheeldon Barn, an' down below 'ere was what they called Edge's Ridge. Some fields 'ave been made bigger, the boundaries 'ave gone.

My brother-in-law, Bill Cope, when 'e left school, went workin' for a nearby farmer an' their milk went down to Ecton Dairy. Some milk was made int' cheese an' some went on the train. Well, some people could be daft an' avaricious; they took the milk down theirselves an' washed the churns out there after they'd tipped the milk. And take churn brush home with 'em. Course the next person ter go along, the churn brush was missin' an' they'd 'ave go an' get another out o'th' stores. Well, Bill was takin' the milk one day an' 'is boss says to 'im, 'Bring churn brush back.' But when 'e came back with horse an' cart, 'Did yer get churn brush?' 'No! I'm not bringin' churn brush.' His boss kicked 'im, so 'e left straight there an' then an' went back t' Reapsmoor, where 'is Dad, Hugh Cope, was joiner and undertaker. 'E went to Shirleys at Waterhouse after; 'e liked it there.

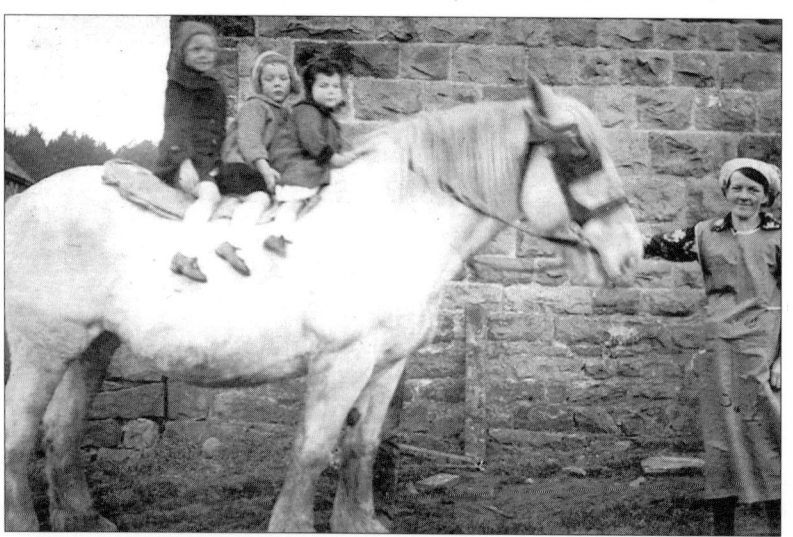

Another tale goin' back; there was a girl; they used call 'er 'flannel' she'd go out at night, milkin' other folk's cows. She 'ad a piece o' flannel in the bottom o' th' bucket, so any one in earshot couldn't 'ear it when she started milkin'.

Another farmer who took 'is milk to Ecton Factory was goin' back up the steep road to Warslow with horse an'

Margaret, Amy (Mum) and Doris with Grandma Gee at Hayes 1922.

cart, bringin' a churn o' milk back that 'e was supposed to 'ave emptied inter the vats. 'E'd either feed some pigs or calves or take it agen next day; 'e didn't intend leavin' it. 'E'd 'ave two or three churns in and this one tipped over, milk spillin' everywhere; that give show away, right off. Somebody in Warslow drew a sketch an' sent it 'em. My dad used say some farmers were their own worst enemy.

Miss Thomas, Manageress
of Ecton Dairy.

Flo Callerdine
at Gollin,
Hollinsclough 1930s.

Sometime around 130 years ago, there was a Johnson lad from Ludburn, who started seein' a girl from Monyash. Course you were on foot weren't y' if y' 'adn't got a bicycle and there were always plenty horses at The Low. Comin' up Low Lane, 'e decided grab one o' these horses - some horses were turned out with 'ead-collars on. Gets on its back an' went fer Monyash. Somebody spotted 'im an' 'e got 'ad up fer stealin'. They 'ad 'im in Derby Crown Court and you could get death sentence or be deported. One of the Goulds, who this horse belonged to, they went t' court an' pleaded with judge not t' give death sentence an' 'e were deported. 'Im an' another bloke were sent Australia. 'E did ever so well an' built a village an' called it Sheen.

Hartington water fountain, Bassett's
Garage on the right.

Sam Johnson 1930s.

Sam Callerdine at Ridge.

Sheen Farmers Tug of war team 1969.
L-R: Stephen Oliver, Philip Boon, Joe Critchlow, Brian Jones, Peter Etches, John Etches, John Critchlow.
Front: David Critchlow, John Shann, Reg Oliver, Roy Simpson, Charlie Critchlow, Wally Street.

Hilda Shann

My father-in-law, John Shann was a descendant of the Gilman family of Sheen. He was born at Gorton in Manchester and after leaving school, he started up as a coal merchant and he ran a removal service.

After the first war, he met and married Martha and joined her at Hill End Farm, Sheen. Later they moved to Cross Farm, where I still live, having married their son John.

My husband was one of the founder members of Sheen Farmers Tug-of-war team in 1968, along with John Critchlow of Manor Farm. He pulled with them for a while before becoming the coach and the team grew and went on to achieve great success winning many National and International titles and World Championships.

For many years, the village held Sheen TOW Day in August to raise money to support the team. Bosley Wood Treatment team were the great rivals and if they didn't come along, it would be a poorer affair.

I think every household in the parish played a part of some kind. We baked lots of cakes and made sandwiches. At Manor farm, Myra cooked massive joints of beef and John Snr sat there all afternoon carving it. My daughter, Lillian always remembers him sharpening his carving knife with the steel to carve those wafer-thin slices.

Lots of sausages were cooked for hot dogs but helpers seemed to be in short supply to prepare the onions, so on the Sunday morning for some years, we would get the kitchen table out onto the yard at Cross Farm and Brenda Oliver, Myrtle and May, myself and Lillian prepared about half a hundredweight of onions. Palins, greengrocers from Matlock used to donate them - the lads did a bit of tugging as well and they also donated a sack of potatoes for the prize draw.

OAKENCLOUGH 1747 (Claude)

When I was researching the history of Oakenclough, I searched the archives at Stafford, Matlock and Burton and found nothing. The maps in the archives at Stafford for this area showed the location of Oakenclough as a blank space. So I turned to some of my historian friends to see what they could suggest as my next move. I had a first recorded mention of Oakenclough in 1405 and some of the older locals claimed the hall had a tower. The present house was built on the site of the old one which burned down between 1885 and 1890. One of my friends suggested that I went to Sheffield Records Office, where I found to my delight a map dated 1747, with an etching of the old hall in the corner and with every field named and numbered including a pindell, which would have been property of the Parish; the hay from which went to feed animals kept in the parish pinfold, which still exists opposite Hocker farm.

I believe the early maps would have been funded by the Harpurs, who owned most of the surrounding area and who wouldn't acknowledge the existence of Oakenclough. In the top right-hand corner of the map, there is a drawing of a church in ruins and also a scroll on which it says, R Newton of Norton. He was the landowner. With finding the map at Sheffield and knowing some history of the Bagshawe family, I thought that he must be a member of that family; whose headquarters and estate offices were at The Oaks, Norton, Sheffield - thus the Norton was there and not the one in Staffordshire.

I also realised that the very name Oakenclough was significant, like Shireoaks near Chapel-en-le-Frith, which my family farmed for 40 years, renting it from the Bagshawe family and Oakenclough near Hayfield on the side of Kinder and several other places with oak in their title, all on the perimeter of the huge Bagshawe estate.

I believe the tower mentioned by the old folks to be the small tower of the church which was in Savage Croft, also on the map. The Savages were foresters and one became Archbishop of York and spent much of his wealth building out-of-the-way churches or chapels. Further evidence of a meeting house is on old maps which show four footpaths leading to the site and a building. Nothing remains except two dressed grit-stone gate stumps now at the entrance to Boarsgrave Farm, removed from Savage Croft.

REAPSMOOR CHEESE FACTORY (Claude)

When I was in Denmark in the late 1940s on a Young Farmers' exchange visit, we were discussing the farm patterns around us on Zeeland. The farm buildings were surrounded by their own fields, all very orderly and the next farm about half a mile away and so on. I asked why it was set out so and they said that after the First War, the farms were in a poor state and the government wanted to modernise farming so that the country economy could prosper.

The powers-that-be looked at what other countries were doing especially Britain. They looked at where farmers were working co-operatively and they told me that the first farm co-operative ventures were the cheese factories of the Peak District . I was surprised when they claimed that the cheese factory at Reapsmoor was the first genuine farmers' Co-operative in the world. One of the farmers from Nordgarden assured me that it was so and when they came over on a farm exchange in 1950, they wanted to look at it.

The farms over there were situated around their own dairy, all within comfortable horse-travelling distance, taking fresh milk into the dairy for butter or cheese and bringing yesterday's skimmed milk or whey back for the pigs. And Denmark is still famous for its butter and its bacon.

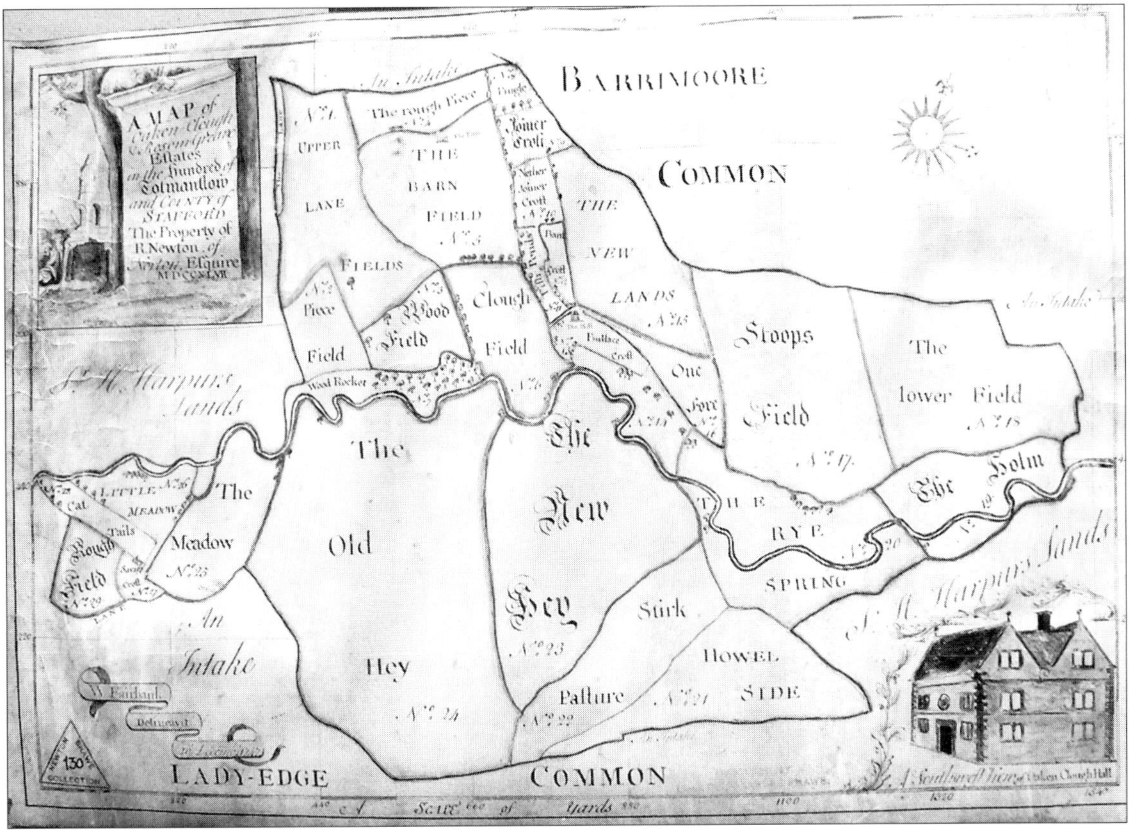

Oakenclough 1747. (Newton Shawe Collection NSC130.)
Reproduced by permission of the Director of Culture, Sheffield City Council

Haymaking at Boosley Grange

William Gould.

Barrow Moor (Golden Green) 1930s.

Below, at Newtown Alan Woolley, Cyril Kirkham, Tommy Oliver, and Finney Oliver.

Joyce Mellor

The Manifold Dairy Cheese Factory on Reapsmoor was opened in 1876. Local farmers, who at that time had difficulty in selling their milk, had decided to build it on land given by the Shirley family. They carted all the stone themselves and also built a cottage below to provide a dwelling for the cheese- maker. My grandfather, William Sutton was born at Hartington in 1866. After leaving school, he worked in a butchers shop in Buxton and took up cheese making in 1888, helped by his brother-in-law, John Woolley of Raikes Farm, Hartington.

After 20 years successful management of the Reapsmoor factory, grandfather was awarded a gold watch by a deputation of Mr William Johnson, Heath House Farm; Mr Arthur Shirley, Rewlach; Mr Samuel Shirley, The Holmes and Mr George Critchlow of Warslow. Mr Sam Shirley is recorded as congratulating grandfather on his *expert knowledge as a cheese- maker and his assiduous attention to his duties for so many years as a result of which the factory was in a most flourishing condition, its products commanding good prices and a quick sale.*

L to R: John Woolley, William Sutton, Ernest Green.

He also made two of what are believed to be the biggest cheeses ever made in England, of 2,000 lbs each. They were exhibited as a Christmas shop window decoration in Mr Ernest Green's shop on St Edwards Street, Leek. Also 2 lesser ones of 1521 and 1542 lbs.

He died in 1923, aged 57, after 35 years service. My father, John had joined after serving in the First War. He worked there for 42 years and was then awarded a gold watch. He won many prizes at local shows and even the London Dairy show.

I was born at Boosley Grange, Newtown, the home of my grandparents, Mr and Mrs Lownds. I lived there for a year, then we moved to the Ferns, then to the Cheese Factory house and from there up to Hillview, which Dad built, then to Broadham Farm, then to here, Grange Lea. I can see all the places where I've lived. I have been on Reapsmoor for 80 years and I've enjoyed it always, especially when the cheese making was going on - all the horses and carts and the farmers coming with the milk and taking the whey.

The family at Boosley for Sunday dinner.
AT VERY BACK: Robert and Colin Lownds. BACK: Ada, Joan & Eric Beresford. Gilbert Lownds.
MIDDLE: Sarah Ann Cooper, Nellie Beresford, Granny Hill (Enoch Hill's, of Halifax B.S. fame, mother),
Grandma Sarah Jane Lownds, Edwin Beresford.
FRONT: Tom Beresford, Fanny Lownds with baby Bobby, Grandad William Lownds & Fred Beresford.

J. Sutton, Albert Mellor, William Gee 1940.

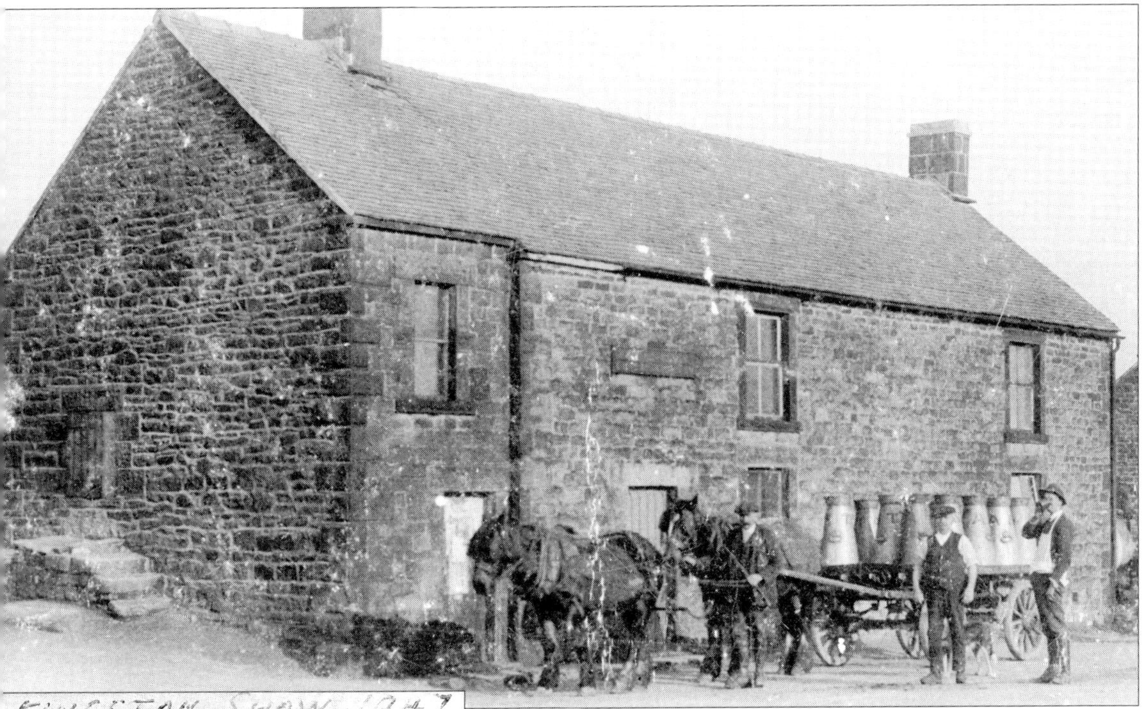

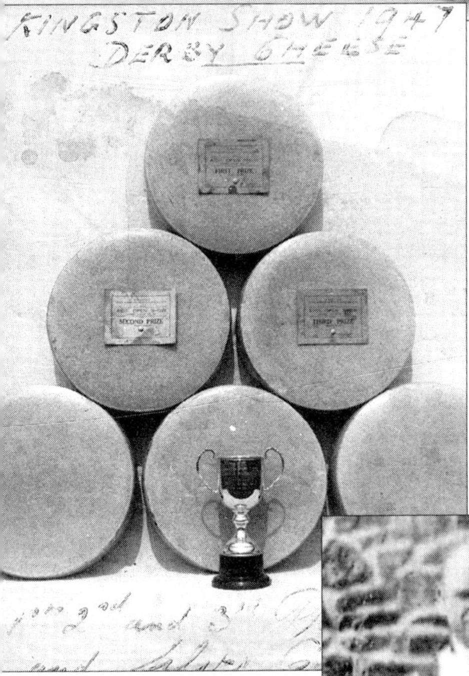
KINGSTON SHOW 1947
DERBY CHEESE
SECOND PRIZE

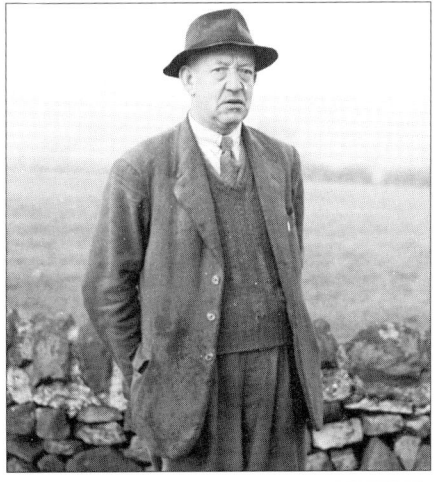

ABOVE:
Reapsmoor Cheese Factory. Grandad Sutton in centre.

J. Sutton (Dad).

LEFT
1st, 2nd and 3rd prize, and silver cup for Derby Cheese.

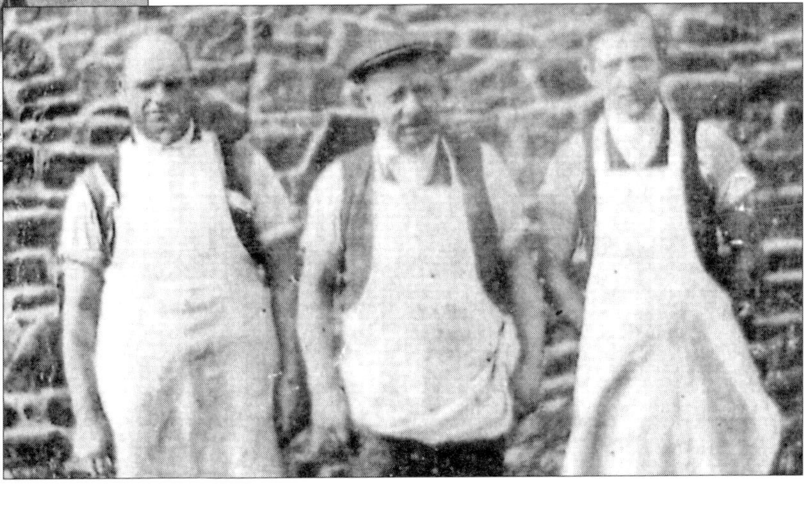

Cheese-makers.

Uncle Colin Lownds helped Dad in the factory until after the War. Others were Isaac Kirkham, Albert Mellor, Dennis Hudson, John Gilman, Uncle Gilbert Lownds and Stan Thompson. They used to call him Steamy Stan, because he used to steam the churns out. Also Joe Grindey and Tom Dainton - all employed at different times.

When we lived at the factory house, we had to be up early in the morning to get the boiler going - an old-fashioned stoke-up boiler. Then the farmers started bringing the milk in with their horse and carts. It was in 17 gallon churns and they tipped them into the weighing pan. Father stood there for hours waiting for the farmers to come; 30 of them. The milk was weighed in pounds by a machine, then the farmers took their churns home to wash them.

The milk then went down a big long fridge, which cooled it when it was going away if they weren't cheesemaking. They didn't make it in winter-time, they didn't like cheese made from stall-fed cattle. Dad worked on Sundays and had 6 weeks off in winter to make up for them, though during that time, he and Uncle Colin thoroughly cleaned and scrubbed the factory through.

Inside the Cheese Factory. Mr Mellor (on the left) of Longnor, known as Glisiker, and Uncle Will Sutton

There were two vats in the factory and I used to like to go and watch the men at work. There was a big thermometer floating about; I've got it now and I used to have a wooden rake and you had to rake it until it was a certain temperature. Dad would say, *'Mind that thermometer,'* in case I broke it - I loved stirring the vat with the wooden rake; I only did it now and again.

Then he put the rennet in and it turned into curd and you ran the whey off. When the whey had all run off, the curd was still very soft and it had to set some more for a while before Dad put a big cut down the middle of the vat, then sliced it each side; he was on one side and Uncle Colin on the other side. Then it had to be turned that way, then the other way, put the salt on, then it was ready for grinding.

Dad knew exactly what to do, he grabbed a handful of curd, I can see him now, and he went to the boiler house and put an iron in the fire, then rubbed the iron on a stone. Then he held this handful of curd against the iron and held them up to the light and he could tell if it was ready for grinding or not. I've watched him do it many a time. Then he'd throw that handful of curd across the road and all the crows came and fetched it.

There was no electric, the grinder ran by steam from the coal-fired boiler. It had to be stoked up and Albert Mellor did a lot of that. It used loads and loads of coal.

Mother and I had to make the cheese-binders; every day they made about 20 cheeses, maybe more if they were Derby cheeses, less if they were the bigger Cheddars. I wanted to go out and play and I couldn't because there were all these binders to be sewn. My friend Enid used to come up, *'Aren't you coming out to play?'* And I couldn't, mother said I had to sew this long string of binders, then we had to cut them with scissors and separate them. The house was full of dust. We set a day a week for it, we never got paid, it came along with Dad's wages, just part of the job.

Mother was a very good cook and was always busy - she had to have dinner ready as they would rush up for their dinner and not have much time to spare when the vats were working quickly.

It was heavy work, lifting the heavy cheese moulds and putting them one on top of another, then wind the press down on them. Then the cheeses had to go down in the drying room and they had to be turned in there. When Dad had finished, at night he had to go up where they were stored and turn them to stop them sticking and to make sure they matured evenly. I used to help him, pass them or roll them to him - these were the Derby cheeses; they were 35 lbs in weight. The Cheddars were turned on racks, they pressed a lever and that turned them.

They made Derby and Cheddar. The Derby cheeses were flatter and stronger tasting; Dad had a borer for testing and he'd say, *'Do you want a little taste?'* and just give me the littlest bit off the end of his finger. It was lovely; there's nothing like it today.

Express Dairies took it over and Dad was put in charge over all the cheese making at Rowsley, Glutton Bridge and Brailsford as well as Reapsmoor. Mr Wall from Rowsley wanted him to make some different cheese, so he brought all this cabbage and greenery for mother and me to put through an ordinary mincer to make this green juice to put in this cheese. I don't know if it was to make Derby Sage. But Dad didn't like doing it; it wasn't his kind of cheese-making he said. Cheese making ended in 1958, the depot finally closed in 1964.

Dad could mend a watch, a weather glass or a grandfather clock and he loved photography - he liked being up on the moors with his camera. One day someone told him that Tommy Phillips was asleep at the side of the road, I think he'd had a few drinks, and Dad ran and fetched his camera and took a photo. Tommy came from Warslow and travelled round with a basket selling reels of cotton, laces and buttons and things. He used to come at Christmas with his mouth-organ and play, *'Will the Angels play their harps for me?'*

I attended Reapsmoor School until I was 9 and also enjoyed the services at Reapsmoor Church when Mr J Lomas, who lived at the Green was the preacher.

My brother, Bernard Sutton was born at the factory house and when the factory closed, he used part of it to keep his coach in. He had his first coach when he was 23 and did school runs and trips and fetched parties of school children from down south up to Hartington Youth Hostel, and took them out to places of local interest. For many years he took a coach load of local people up to Scotland for their holidays, staying at different hotels. He was always very popular.

This is a poem that we found in Dad's jacket pocket; we think it's about 100 years old:

BUTCHER'S ARMS INN

Kind friends just pay attention
And listen for a while
To the doings up at Reapsmoor pub
And I think that you will smile.

At 8 o'clock we start the ball
Presided o'er by Thomas Hall
A jolly fellow full of life
And wanting nothing but a wife.

His right-hand friend, John from The Lowe
Is never absent, rain or snow.
The drops of whisky he has drank
Would nicely fill the factory tank

Give order please and you shall hear
The finest voices strong and clear
From tenor high to bass quite low
They can't be beat where'er you go.

I give first call on Mossy Joe
That singer great as you all know.
With head erect and clos'ed eyes
He nearly makes the ceiling rise.

A hearty clap and stamp of feet
And Joseph drops into his seat.
'Tha did that well' says Harry Plant
'Some more like tha's just what we want.'

Next comes the tenor Tommy Lock
With voice just like a bantam cock.
But like his songs there is no doubt
That his old voice is quite worn out.

Tis ten o'clock and the night is dark
But we get a light thanks to old sparks
Filled to the top with ten-penny beer
We find it hard our loads to steer.

So was the time at Reapsmoor spent
A place where I one night once went.
And if for singing you have a whim
Just spend one night
            at the Butcher's Arms Inn.

Tommy Phillips

Grandad Lownds, Dad and Uncle Bob in the background.

Bernard Sutton around 1940.

Harold Halsey, Bernard Sutton, Kathleen Fletcher, Joyce Sutton, Betty Sutton, John Sutton, Norman Halsey.

Mowing at Boosley Grange

Haymaking at Boosley Grange

Haymaking at Boosley Grange

No. 17 Platoon 'C' Coy Leek battalion Home Guard. Dec 1944.

BACK: Privates I. Wood, A. Woolley, A.J. Titterton, G. Bradbury, P. Lownds, G.H. Shenton, B. Riley, E. Howson, W.T. Riley, C. Mellor, G.G. Mellor, T.C. Clapham, T.I. Johnson, E. Swindells.

MIDDLE: Privates J. Hall, J.R. Gee, F. Broomhead, K.G. Wooliscroft, G. Gee, J. Mellor, R. Keeling, I. Gee, I. Gee, J.W. Alcock, W.T. Swindells, F. Barker, B. Barker, A. Lomas.

FRONT: Privates W. Shenton, L/Cpl J. Lomas, L/Cpl J. Gilman, Cpl A. Cope, Sgt A. Grindon, Lieut. W. Heath, Sgt F. Allen, Cpl J. Gee, Cpl J.E. Sutton, Cpl G. Sutton, Pte R. Lownds.

John Mellor

I was born at School Clough, the fifth of 11 children. When I was 8 years old, we were playing in the farmyard and I got a bit too near the shippon door and my Dad presented me with a bucket and stool and I milked my first cow.

When I was 10 years old, I remember a cattle dealer from the Leek area, Isaac Brunt came to buy some cows and they finally agreed on £8 apiece for two cows, but they had to be delivered to the Mermaid Inn on the following Saturday at the price. He'd got a very clean new suit on and I think my Dad taunted him a bit about it, saying he'd be better off than Dad, but they agreed on the price and he put his hand in a deep pocket in the front of his trousers and pulled a roll of white five pound notes out. He gave him three of them and one gold sovereign - £16; we thought he was the Bank of England, because we were only used to pennies - we had a Saturday penny, that was our pocket money.

We took these cows up to the Mermaid, met Isaac Brunt and his drover and they took them onto Leek and my Dad followed up with pony and trap to bring us home.

I was in to rabbitin' with ferrets. I made a ferret hutch out of a well-used, unwanted crate that my uncle, Charlie Batkin brought me from Hindlow station. I made it into a hutch on legs. Saturday was the only day that mattered, I used to come back loaded with as many rabbits as I could carry; I was between 11 and 14 then. Once I was crossing the road with my load of rabbits and there were some council men working on the road. One said, *'Wut sell me a rabbit?'* I said, *'Yes, one rabbit - one shilling.'* I remember his nickname - Ginger Wain. A deal was done.

As time went by father gave up driving to Leek with the pony and trap. Byrne's bus started a service from Longnor to Leek and we used to take him to meet the bus at Millmoor Head junction in the morning and meet him off the bus in the afternoon with all the shopping.

John

At School Clough,
William Bradbury and
Linda Mellor 1950.

Below: Flood at
Blakebrook July 17th
1956, after cloudburst
above Fleet Green.

Reservoir Protest.
Walter Cundy and
George Deaville
on the right.

1933 was a special year for me; on the 24th February there was a very bad blizzard, it had been freezing for a week, the ground was rock hard. We were all playing at school and it started snowing at 3 o'clock and we had to be fetched home by pony and float by John Kirkham, who was the waggoner at School Clough at the time. It snowed until Sunday afternoon, 4 o'clock, never stopped. Not only were the roads blocked, but there was three foot of snow in the fields. The biggest three day snow I've ever seen in my life.

In March the Milk Marketing Board was formed, which was the best thing that ever happened to farmers. And I left school in December - three memorable things in 1933.

I got more fond of horses than cows and I started being the waggoner when Mr Kirkham left. I loved ploughing, mowing, binding, anything to do with horses. I never walked home when I'd done a job; I could jump on one of the horse's backs off the floor and sit on sideways.

I cut most of the corn locally with the binder; a Massey-Harris binder and three horses. We didn't charge much; about a pound an acre for cutting and binding the corn. I made my own swingle-tree for the binder out of a three inch square by ten foot long piece of oak to fit the three horses side by side. Some people would put one on the front but I thought they were better side by side; I could drive them myself; it needed another man if you had one in front to ride on its back. I did that before I went school; if they were mowing I used give 'em a pull up Big Meadow. My Dad would say, 'Come on lad, it's time thee were goin' on thee bike, its ten t' nine.' We had to milk before we went to school; two sisters and my elder brother, Ben - two or three each.

There came a man to Bakewell with two David Brown tractors, £240 a piece. We were looking at them- we were very interested and my Dad said, 'Let's go lad afore we do summat daft. Thayt a good ploughman, thay con plough wi'out a tractor.'

Eventually people went onto tractors, they didn't need ungearing. This binder job, when you got to the field, you'd got three horses in and geared them up and hitched them up to the binder. You'd get there and there comes a shower. Then you would have to take them back, ungear them and let them out again. That was what happened many a time.

I'd go to the blacksmith at Shining Ford; it's altered out of all recognition now. It cost £1 for 4 new shoes. It was a lovely place to go; I spent hours and hours there. I used take a young horse and you put a twitch on his nose to stop him kicking; a short piece of wood with a loop on and you put it round his nose and when he'd attempt a kick, give it another twist to give him something to think about. Or you could pick the front leg up and put a strap round it. They soon got used to it.

Every village had its own parson in those days and in October 1937, Sheen parson was taking the Harvest festival service at Newtown Church. The church was full of farmers and smallholders and during his sermon he said there were two things he had never seen in his life; a satisfied farmer and a dead donkey! And also that Sheen farmers spent a lot of their time leaning over gates talking and smoking their pipes.

The next event on the calendar was Sheen Wakes dance round about the end of October; I presumed the proceeds were for the parson. Brother Ben and me went to the dance in father's new Austin 12 car. We parked in Shann's farm yard opposite from Sheen school, where the dance was. We thought it would be safe there.

When we came out, we found all our tyres, including the spare wheel were flat and punctured. All the cars in the car park had also got flat tyres. We were lucky; there was an old bath full of water, which helped us find where the punctures were and we'd all the tackle to mend them, including hand pump and flash light. We mended four and finally got home and to bed by four o'clock in the morning. At half past six, Father said, *'Come on my lads, if you can be men at night, you must be men in a morning.'*

There were two brothers living in Longnor, Jim and Wilfred Needham. Jim worked at Folds End and Wilfred used to run a taxi before anybody else had got a motor in the 1920s. It was an old Ford, a tall one. I remember we would go and stay with our uncle and aunty at Dale Gap Farm at Rocester - go on the bus and Wilfred would fetch us back. We came back the last week in August, before Longnor Wakes Sunday, the first week in September.

Longnor Wakes Sunday was quite a big occasion for our family. Many a time with us younger children, there'd be 20 people for dinner. We had a big mahogany table and we had to wind it out and put a big leaf in the middle to make it bigger. We'd have a big lump of beef, bigger than a large loaf and then plum pudding and rum dip. Nice for some people, but a lot of work for my mother and my two eldest sisters, Emma and Anne.

Just a few recollections on the very cold winter of 1947, before global warming! I had previously made a horse-drawn sledge with the help of our blacksmith, Mr Jack Bradbury at Shining Ford. He made me some steel runners out of a hoop off a one-horse cart wheel and all the other fittings. I bolted the shafts on, off the Blackstone side rake. On the 5th Feb, we had three days milk in at School Clough; all the roads were blocked after a very bad blizzard on 2nd Feb. We had a very good young horse; we loaded as many churns as we could get in the sledge, along with shovels and wire-cutters and set off for Reapsmoor Cheese factory down the fields. Down our 20 acre meadow, cut the wire fence into Mr Arthur Gee's field at The Ridge, cut the wire on both sides of the road and down through Gee's farmyard. Then carried on to the bottom of his meadows and cut the fence into Mr George Lowe's field at The Holmes, crossed the river and up through his farmyard and up the field to the cheese factory.

Owing to continuous snow storms and a strong east wind, most roads were still blocked and we took our milk on this track, other farmers as well, until the 13th March. All work on the farm was done by horses; hay had to be got in from stacks in the fields, there were no such things as bales or silage bales. We fetched our corn from Longnor, Mr Charlie Batkin's, and groceries from his shop after making a track through Mr Kidd's Brownspit land. Of course, that was when there was some to fetch, it was a good while before there was. In the spring, we had to repair all the fences.

In the 1960s, the Trent River Authority proposed to construct a reservoir in the Manifold Valley south of Longnor. It would have been within 250yards of Longnor market square and been $2^1/2$ miles long, covering 1,100 acres. The dam would have been at Rewlach. 33 farms would have been affected; the land where I live would have been under water. We formed a committee to fight it: myself, K Critchlow, Sheen: George Deaville, Sam Kidd snr, Jim Critchlow, Boothlow: Bill Johnson, Bill Gould. Walter Cundy, Lower House Farm was chairman, John Gould, Folds End was vice-chairman, Stuart Worthington, Swainsley was secretary and Henry Johnson, treasurer. We raised a substantial fighting fund through local events and donations and produced a booklet with a foreword by Sir John Betjeman. We finally went to London to lobby in the House of Commons. The plan was abandoned in 1972 in favour of Carsington.

Tom Critchlow

I've lived in Sheen parish all my life, until we retired to Leek 9 years ago. I was born at Lower Boothlow in 1927. We moved up to Over Boothlow when I was about 2 years old. My parents had married in 1916 and been at Lower Boothlow, which was rented, then when Over Boothlow became vacant, they bought it. Someone else rented Lower Boothlow for 7 years, then father took the tenancy over again. He bought Low End in 1942.

I went to Longnor school mostly except when I stayed at my grandfather's farm, Pump Farm at Warslow, from December 1939 to June 1940, when I attended Warslow school. I had to go back home when Dad broke his leg. Him and a neighbour, they were just cornerin' a cow to draw her out, on a little bit o' land at bottom o' Knowsley there. She turned quick and knocked me Dad down; he didn't even know he'd bin trodden on, till he looked down at his feet and saw one facin' the other way. It were broken in two places and he was in plaster about 17 weeks.

Easter 1941, I went to work for my uncle at Brund for 18 months, then back to Boothlow ready for the move to Low End in 1943, with Dad, mother and Hilda. My older brothers and sisters stayed farming the two Boothlows. There were 7 of us; Jim, Gilbert, Septimus, Catherine (Kitty), Mariah, me and Hilda.

Father used to rear Shorthorn bulls and he treated himself to a pair of horn-trainers; I have a nice set here. The two ends are open-ended cups made of lead, connected by two adjustable leather straps. They train the horns to grow correctly or as you wanted them. They say that light attracts horns and if the bulls were tied in a dark shed, perhaps with light at one end, the horns might grow forward. You liked them just on the curve forward and slightly up. If they grew upwards too much, they were like cow horns. You'd perhaps keep them on a few months. Of course you don't see many horns on bulls these days, they're all dehorned.

We also had a set of trusses, which were put on a cow after she'd calved, to prevent her putting her calf-bed out. It was made of canvas with leather straps. Dad could put a calf-bed back again; today, you'd send for the vet. I know when I was a lad, on one occasion at Boothlow, a cow had calved and put her bed out and father had put it back. He said we'd better look at this other cow which had calved and she'd put hers out too. He couldn't face another and sent for Mr Kidd at Brownspit to do it.

Mother was a Bonsall, from West Side at Hulme End and she had two brothers. Through them, I have two ledgers which belonged to this chap, Ralph Twigg, who got his living as a sadler up the back of Ecton. He married Hannah Critchlow.

Various entries:

1891 Joseph Baker, Wetton—lining donkey collar	1s	9d
1891 Fred Yates - new leathering bellows	1s	
1892 Enoch Barker - new pair leggings	8s	
1892 John Brindley - new pair braces	2s	
1895 Billy Shipley - new whip lash		6d
1895 Adolphus Lomas, Hartington-new pair hacking bridles	7s	6d
1895 Ralph Wood - mending dog muzzle		6d
1896 Thomas Sutton - new hedge mittens	1s	9d
1896 Mr Lomas, Reapsmoor - new cart saddle, crupper and breeching	£2 10s	
1897 George Green - new kicking strap	2s	3d
1898 Sampson Barker - new calf muzzle		9d
2 calf skins were offset on someone's account	5s	6d
1886 Mr William Finney, Ecton - new whip lash		3d

John Bonsall on the left working out of Ecton Quarry in the 1920s.

BELOW:
The Thompson family at Waterslacks in Butterton 1920s.

2 pennyworth of oil	2d
New head-collar and chain	6s
New piece of leather for horses foot	3d
Mr Joseph Weston, Ecton-new collar and housing	18s 6d
1 bottle embrocation	2s
1895 Mr C Finney, Cawlow - leather for trap shafts	2s 6d
4 washers for trap	1s
1886 Sir Vauncey Crew - lapping whip	6d
New lash for carriage whip	1s 6d

Sir Vauncey

The entries for the whips for Sir Vauncey should have been 3d but were crossed out and changed to 6d when they saw who was paying. He also supplied oil to Ecton mines, sometimes written *point of oile, and weshers*, which may have been the leather washers for pumps.

When you go to a farm sale nowadays, there's all the machinery to look at. In those days, one of the first things you looked at was the cart saddle and gearing for the horses if it needed replacing. Or you looked for a milk unit; you might have three and you could do with another.

You'd have a horse with a foal and in summertime you'd fetch them both in, shut the foal up and take the mare haymakin'. When you got back, the first job was, you ungeared the horse, then you went in the house for some nice chilled water and you washed her udder before you let the foal to it. They reckoned in them days that the milk would be too warm with her working and sweating and could give the foal stomach ache or colic. But the last one at Low End, it got as it wouldn't come inside, it stopped out in the field. But as soon as you landed in the yard with the mother from haymaking' teddin' whatever, it come and helped itself, we hadn't time wash her and it never took any harm.

Our main income at Low End was always milk. We had quite a lot of hens and pigs at one time when there was money in them. We were one of the first in the area to breed Suffolk sheep; during the War a big carcass was preferred which in a lot of cases the Oxford provided. My brother and myself were interested and Mr Mosley from Bakewell got us the first one. I think the only other person in the area to keep registered Suffolks was Mr Charlie Prince who kept the New Inns Hotel on the Ashbourne road. We thought that they produced a leaner carcass than the Oxford. Then of course every one went on to them.

My brother Jim always did the ploughing; we had a wooden plough which is still at Low End. It's had a fresh coulter, a disc which made it easier to cut turf. We did bits before the War, but then you had to plough more in wartime and both Boothlows together were over 200 acres. There might have been 15 acres under the plough and he did it all with the single furrow wooden plough and two horses.

I was ploughing with two horses one day at Low End on sandstone. Bill Johnson used

At Villa Farm, Warslow 1930s.

At Westside Mill.
Ann Coates, John Gould, Joyce Gould, and above Tony France. 1950s.

George Grindon Critchlow, Low End,
late 1950s.

James Critchlow at Waterhouse Yard, late 1960s.

Uncle Richard Bonsall using a Bamlett mower at Westside 1940s.

The Thompson family at Dale Farm in the Manifold Valley.

BELOW
Mr Grindey at Broad Ecton.

Ecton Lea

to come and stay and he was following me one day, walking right behind. I said, *'I wouldn't get too close, the shafts may go up in the air if the plough-share hits a stone.'* No sooner had I said it, than up they went and fortunately with being aware, he wasn't too close. Naturally the horses stopped. If you weren't aware, you could get hurt, they went up so quickly and could come down and hit you on top of the head before you realised.

A bit of poetry concerning the war which I know by heart:

> They used to say that England was the land of all the free,
> To say that England never would be slaves.
> They used to boast and swagger what a happy lot were we.
> They used to sing Britannia Rules the Waves.
>
> But when that food controlling started, rationing begun,
> And they commenced to give us coupons for our meals.
> We all got so confused; that at times we didn't know
> Whether we were standing on our head or on our heels.
>
> But we sang Hoorah for England, we gave a mighty cheer
> Our navy held the water and the army drank the beer.
>
> There were coupons for our sugar and coupons for our tea.
> It did cause us all a lot of pain and grief.
> And a soldier home from France one week, he wrecked a grocers shop,
> When he found he wanted one for Bully Beef.
>
> We found this coupon system ruling all our daily lives,
> For when into the barbers shop we'd go
> If we hadn't got a coupon, he'd refuse to cut our hair
> Though he'd sooner charge us a bob and let us go.
>
> According to the papers, they were going to ration girls.
> The allocation we were told was six a week.
> We'd got to prove we were single men before we got our cards.
> The authorities, they had an awful cheek.
>
> Six girls a week my merry lads, it really was hard lines,
> And the prospect didn't look too bright.
> But I know a lot of fellows and I was perhaps one,
> Who could use his coupons up on Sunday night.
>
> A young man and a girl I knew both wanted to get wed.
> But the vicar wouldn't make them man and wife.
> She hadn't got a coupon which permitted her to do so.
> Now that poor girl, she'll be single all her life.
>
> I think the limit it was reached, for I was told one night
> By a friend of mine, whose name was Mr Dun.
> His wife had twins and then they went and fined her fifty pounds
> Cause her coupon just entitled her to one.
>
> But we sang Hoorah for England, we gave a mighty cheer.
> Her navy held the water and the army drank the beer.

At West Side, Hulme End.

In the Manifold Valley.

Billy Gregory, Mary Bonsall, Lizzy Thompson, John Thompson at East Ecton 1928.

O. Bonsall, J. Bonsall, Cissie Cox, Ken Wood at Lees Farm, Ecton 1920s.

Jim and Nancy Coates, Timothy Grant, Ann Coates, Matthew Redfern, Ecton late 1950s.

Local trip early 1950s.
BACK: Mrs Dorothy Smalley, Ted Smalley, - -, - -, Mrs Birch, Mrs Grindon, Mrs Lowe, Alice Bassett,
Mary Bonsall, Mrs Brindley, Mabel Grindey, Tom Bassett.
MIDDLE: Charlotte Wood, Lizzie Thompson, Isaac Gilman, Mrs Gilman, George Birch, Dorothy Deaville,
Ettie Critchlow, - -, Mrs Shirley, Mrs Wain, Mr Smalley, Bob Bury?, John Bonsall,.
SITTING: Kathleen Mellor, Bev. Grindey, Jess Grindey, Mr & Mrs Fallowes, Mrs Shaw,
Ralph Derbyshire, Mrs Derbyshire, Mary Grindey?
FRONT The driver and Ken Mellor.

MINISTRY OF FOOD.

C) 660749   SUGAR
REGISTRATION CARD.

This part to be kept by the Householder.

C. Name .....Miss M. Thompson..........

Address.....Beton..........

.....Wetton..........

.....Ashbourne..........

Retailer with whom the Householder has registered:—

D. Signature of } ....J. A. Thornton..........
Retailer

Address.....Hulme End, Hartington..........

.....Buxton..........

/.... No. of persons....one.......... Initials....b.(W.)

District .....MAYFIELD RURAL DISTRICT COUNCIL..........

S. 2.

BEFORE December 30th, 1917, the supplies of sugar at the shop where you have registered may not be sufficient for you to buy sugar there.

AFTER December 30th, 1917, you should be able to buy at the shop where you have registered the authorised weekly allowance of sugar for your household. You must then be prepared to produce this part of your card whenever required to do so by the retailer named upon it.

If, after December 30th, you have any difficulty in buying this weekly allowance from your retailer, you should communicate with your Local Food Office.

NOTE:—It will be your duty in case of a reduction in the number of your household, to make a corresponding reduction in your purchases of sugar. In case of any increase of household, your retailer will as far as possible allow a corresponding increase in your supplies.

CAUTION.—Any person altering any entries made by the Local Food Office on this card is liable on conviction to a fine not exceeding £100 or 6 months' imprisonment, or both.

Ellen Critchlow

I came from Ford and was a child during the war. I remember when I was about 10, all the farmers had gone to a farm a mile away one night to help rescue a horse from a bog. There were only nine houses at Ford, mostly farms and most had children; there were six of us. The German bombers 'were coming over, an awful drone, we were terrified. There was a bomb dropped at Berkamsytch and one at Grindon Moor - we heard it drop. You could hear it whistle as it came down, then the terrific bang. We were worried for our fathers. Luckily, they all came back safe. In the daytime, there were sometimes droves of aircraft going over, maybe 70 as we were going home from school. They were our planes, I should think coming back from bombing.

I was at Low End for 45 years. The first years seemed very busy; I had four little girls in four years. We'd no electricity then, it was all dolly tub, dolly peg and copper. We had a trough of spring water on the door-stones and had to carry it into the house to the side boiler on the range. Tom's sister, Hilda helped on a Monday with the washing, and on a Friday with the baking, for three years until she got married. We had no fridges of course, but a good cold pantry. We cooked a big joint of meat, about 7 lbs for Sunday dinner; then you had it for Monday dinner then made a meat and potato pie or stew with what was left for Wednesday dinner. There were two work lads living with us and we had three more children - 11 of us to cook for.

When we killed a pig, I made 'hackin'. You used the pluck - the lights, liver and heart. I boiled them up in the piece. You'd probably need two pans, because the lights expand as they cook. Then you had to take all the pipes out of the lights and chop everything up finely. I cut the fat up into cubes about as big as a dice and rendered it down to make the lard, which left the scratchings. I mixed them with the meat, a bit of lard, some of the juices from the boiling, and salt and pepper. You then had a soft paste which you put into a dish or basin to set. We always had it on toast; it was between a pate and brawn, very rich,

I also made savoury ducks, which I liked better. You used a half loaf of bread or more, onions, chopped and boiled, lean pork steak, cut up fine and cooked liver, cut up fine. Then season with salt, pepper, thyme and perhaps a pinch of sage. Then into balls and you cut a piece of the 'shawl' of the pig and wrapped each ball in that, or you could do it in a roasting tin.

Kathleen Bassett at Low End 1950.

PARISH QUARRIES (Claude)

In 1991, I was selected to serve on Heathylee Parish Council. The first meeting that I attended was held in one of the admin offices at the army camp on Blackshaw moor. I was welcomed by the chairman, who then opened up the meeting; but not knowing the background to the business at hand, it was of little interest to me until the clerk read a letter from the Peak District National Park stating that they were going to landscape and put gates on Pethills Quarry, with keys being held by the County Council and the PDNP.

Some of the councillors said that the quarry had been used by local farmers for the storing and exchange of produce, for instance when the minor roads were impassable due to snow, the farmers could meet the milk wagon with their horse and sledge or later tractors, also picking up coal, corn, hay or groceries. But with locked gates and no keys for the parish council, they would lose the use of this valuable asset.

After further discussions, it was decided that as the Peak Park were now the owners of the Warslow Moors Estate, there was not much that we could do about it. With this being my first meeting, I said nothing, but I thought a lot - memory bells were ringing. My father had worked on 6 or 7 quarries, but not a parish quarry, so it had to be Grandad. It was a story I had listened to as a child, when there was no wireless or TV; people made their own entertainment, story telling or singing. For me it was always a great day when Grandad came to stay and we'd spend the evening listening to his stories.

One story that he related was when he left Whiston, where he was living with his grandma and walked to Fairfield, Buxton to look for work. He'd be about 20 and had already been to Stafford and Leek. On the way to Buxton, as he passed the Royal Cottage pub, men were sat at a table outside drinking. He realised he couldn't buy a drink; he'd spent his last money at Leek buying bread and cheese. So he needed to earn a bit of money quick; the Derbyshire border was only 2 miles away and it was a favourite meeting place for police looking for vagrants - which without money in his pocket, Grandad was.

So after about half a mile, he met two men with a horse and cart, who were mending pot-holes with broken stone. He asked them if they knew anywhere that he could earn a few coppers to put him on his way. One replied, *'There's always work in the parish quarry napping stone.'* Grandad said he would call at the quarry whereupon one of the men rooted in the cart tool box and came out with a strange looking hammer with a round head used for napping. He lent it to Grandad saying, *'You have to have your own hammer, you should be alright now, the quarry is quarter of a mile up the road.'* Which would make it Pethills Quarry.

So he went on his way and found the quarry, where two men sat breaking stone down into small pieces. Another man sat on the wall, he turned out to be the road foreman responsible for who did what, the size of the stone being broken and the hours that the men with the horse and cart did.

When Grandad asked him for a job, he took him to a heap of stone and left him to get on with it. Eventually the other two men came back and it being close to finishing time, the foreman signed their notes so that they could go home. Before they left, one of them gave Grandad a small parcel which turned out to be a good thick cheese sandwich. As the other two stone-breakers got ready for going, the foreman asked Grandad how long he was *stopping.* *''Til I've earned half a crown.'* He replied. *'Good, you can shelter in my cabin overnight; there's a stove in there and kettle. You can make a mug of tea.'* Then he left.

As it got darker, Grandad stopped work, looked at his sandwich, went in the cabin, got the fire going and the kettle on. He said he could still taste the sandwich, it was so good. Then he slept in the hut and at first light went back to breaking stone. By the time the men with the cart came and the foreman, he had a good heap of stone broken, which the foreman asked the men to load onto their cart. He said it was a good even load and he paid grandad, who asked for it in small change, so he could pay the man for the sandwich and the ganger for the tea. The foreman said, *'Don't worry about paying, I'll do it and tell them you offered.'* He sent him on his way with *'the best of luck!'*

John Thompson, - -, John Wood,
Sid Shipley, Ecton Quarry

Grandad carried on to some relations at Tomthorn, Fairfield and after about a year, he married their daughter at Fairfield Church in 1904. In 2004, my granddaughter moved into the same house that Grandad moved into on his marriage.

His story came back to me and it gave me inspiration to research and later fight the PDNP as to the ownership

Crusher at Ecton Quarry 1920s.
John Bonsall, Andrew Barker, Monsal Barker.

of the quarry and various others. I claimed it for the parish and officers at the National park claimed it was theirs. They had documents which looked as though they owned the land when most of the Harpur-Crewe estate was transferred to the Peak Park. But I had documents which demonstrated that pieces of land were awarded to the surveyor of highways of various parishes in 1839 under the terms of the Alstonefield Enclosure Award, and not to the Lord of the Manor. This showed that the land had neither previously nor subsequently been in the possession of the Crewe and Harpur Estate and so it was not theirs to hand over. This took 8 years to be sorted out, eventually being resolved amicably and the land remains the property of the parish.

Graham Mellor

My great grandfather, Benjamin Mellor was born in 1828 and married great-grandma, Ann Atkin, at Biggin Church in 1856. They had 22 children of which 17 survived. 3 died at birth and 2 in early childhood. My grandfather, Clement Valentine was the youngest, born on Valentines Day 1882.

The children were going to Biggin School and grandfather was 3 years old and carried to school on the shoulders of one or other of his brothers. One day he learned that the others in his class had started school at the age of 5 years, so he refused to go again until he was 5 on Feb. 14th 1887. By this time, it was to Reapsmoor School as the family had moved to School Clough Farm. The farm was rented from the Crewe and Harpur Estate and was a big farm of 200 acres including The Green Farm over the road.

In the *Sheffield Weekly Telegraph* of May 24th 1890, there is an article where Great-grandma Ann won a competition for the largest family and was awarded two guineas.

The family all dined together on Good Friday last (including the two young men from the States), at Schoolclough; all healthy and well. Mr Mellor is a grand type of an English farmer and yeoman, and Mrs M is the model of a good wife and mother.

BACK: Charles Septimus, Herbert Henry, Albert Joseph, George Frederick, Benjamin Prince, Edward William, John Thomas.
MIDDLE: Martha, Sarah Ann, Ann Mellor, Clement Valentine, Benjamin Mellor, Mary Jane, Elizabeth Anna.
FRONT: James Edwin, Christopher Victor, Henrietta, Emma, Ernest Alfred.

In 1912, 8 years after Benjamin's death, everything at School Clough had to be sold and Clement had to buy anything that he wanted to carry on farming on the farm. It was held over two days, the livestock and tackle one day and the household furniture and effects 3 days later.

My father, Bert is the youngest of 11 and I am the youngest of 4; so I am the youngest of the youngest of the youngest and am now living at School Clough with my young family.

Father tells us stories of wartime here. The Germans dropped lots of incendiaries - little fire-bombs to try and set places on fire and light the way for the bombers. They were perhaps after the ammunition dumps nearer to Buxton. There were hundreds dropped in the fields some nights. A little heap of white ash was left when they had burned. If they hadn't gone off, the children picked them up and would go climbing trees or on buildings to throw them down and try and get them to go off. Later on, when the Americans came, they gathered them up and made them safe.

The Americans took these plantations over; they were camping in Back Lane woods for weeks and one morning the family here got up to find them camped in the yard, in the buildings, everywhere. There was a little wooden shed, which corn was stored in and they were shaving in there - it was wintertime. There were tanks and vehicles everywhere and they had to work round them for a day or two. I think it was an exercise preparing to take things over. There were half-tracked vehicles all over the fields and anywhere there was a clump of trees they camped, camouflaged.

There was a little plane landed up the field with something wrong once. Uncle John was in the Home Guard, the Butchers Arms was the headquarters. He thought it might be a German plane and grabbed his gun and went creeping up the wall side until he could see that it wasn't. On several occasions during the war, small planes landed in the Square Hill field, as it was known. They were able to land and take off again.

John Woolley

My great grandad, Fred Woolley, married Maude Mary Mellor, Edward William's daughter. Fred's sister, Annie, married Clement. So Grandad Woolley's sister was Granny Woolley's aunty.

Fred came from The Bank at Newtown, but he and Maude were in service at School Clough, so they were married from there on December 13th 1910. On the same day they travelled to Stowe-by-Chartley to where Fred had got a job as a waggoner. On the way they had stopped at Uttoxeter to buy some furniture. The photo shows Fred on the left on a shoot at Amerton Farm, one of the farms he worked on.

Please bring this Catalogue with you to the Sale.

SCHOOL CLOUGH FARM.
LONGNOR.

8 miles from Leek, 8 from Buxton and 13 miles from Ashbourne, 2 miles from Hulme End Station (Manifold Valley Light Railway), 3 miles each from Hurdlow and Hindlow Stations and $4\frac{1}{2}$ miles from Hartington Station, L. & N. Western Railway

W. S. BAGSHAW AND SONS,

have received instructions from the Executors of the late Mr. Benjamin Mellor, to Sell by Auction entirely without reserve, on

TUESDAY, OCT. 29TH, 1912.

The Whole of the very choice and valuable Live and Dead Farming Stock, comprising:—

80 BEASTS

52 SHROPSHIRE SHEEP.

11 HORSES & COLTS

16 GRAND PIGS

A large Collection of Modern

IMPLEMENTS AND TACKLE

DAIRY VESSELS.

3 Stacks of Well-harvested Oats. Quantity of Eating Potatoes. 45 Couples of Fowls and Effects.

Sale to commence at 11 o'clock prompt.

J. H. Henstock, Typ., Ashbourne.

W. S. Bagshaw and Sons, Auctioneers.

74 and 75.	Ditto.	Ditto.
76 and 77.	Ditto.	Ditto.
78 and 79.	Ditto.	Ditto.

80. Reared Red Pedigree Bull Calf.

Horses.

1. Black Shire Mare, 8 years old, 16.1 h.h., Quiet and Good Worker. Sire *Rokeby Friar* 14827, dam by *Don Carlos.* Stinted to *Sheen Redlynch* on June 7.

2. Chestnut Mare, 8 years old, 16.1 h.h. Quiet and a Good Worker in all gears. Sire, *Black Prince.* Dam by *Chief Commander,* grand dam by *Fawfield Head Waggoner.* Stinted to *Foxlow Albert* on May 22nd.

3. CHESTNUT FILLY, 3 years old, 15.3 h.h., quiet and a good worker. Dam No. 1.

4. CHESTNUT COLT, 3 years old, 15.3 h.h., quiet and a good worker in all gears. Sire *Alderfitz, James,* dam by *Don Carlos.*

5. BROWN COB Mare, 5 years old, 14.2 h.h., quiet to ride and drive and very fast. Sire *Golden Rule.*

6. BROWN COB, rising 3, broken to saddle. Sire *Golden Rule.*

7. CHESTNUT FILLY, rising 3, unbroken.

8. BROWN HALF-LEGGED MARE, 10 years old, 14.3 h.h., quiet to ride and drive.

9. GREY FILLY FOAL at Foot of No. 8 by *Foxlow Albert.*

10. BROWN FILLY FOAL, Sire *Kingsway,* dam No. 1.

11. BROWN FILLY FOAL, Sire *Foxlow Albert,* dam No. 3.

Arrangements and Remarks.

Luncheon will be provided by Mr. Ralph Bassett, Light Railway Hotel, at a charge of 1s. 6d. each, returned to purchasers of £2 and over on day of Sale only.

Brakes will meet the morning Trains at Hurdlow Station, L. and N.W. Railway, and Hulme End Station (Manifold Valley Light Railway).

The Auctioneers wish to draw the attention of the Public to this highly important unreserved Sale. The Cattle are all Home Bred, the Dairy Cows are Young, big framed, full of Hair, good milkers and right and straight in their Bags. The Young Stock are all strong good sorts, and having been summered on the Hills will improve when taken away.

The Sheep and Lambs are a grand level lot and coming off sound high Land are well worth attention.

The Horses are well known and are good workers, and include two useful Shire Mares and several promising Fillies and Colts.

The Pigs include Six Beautiful Quality Fat Hogs and Gilts.

Many of the Implements are new and the whole are in capital condition.

Order of Sale :

Implements at 11 prompt, followed by Tackle, Dairy Vessels, Sheep, Pigs, Cattle, Horses, Produce, and Poultry.

CATALOGUE.

Implements.

Quantity of Old Iron.
Quantity of Firewood.
Four Milking Stools.
Three ditto.
Several Swill Tubs.
Turnip Hoes.
Several Cambrels.
Thistle Spuds.
Two Iron Crowbars.
Three Shovels.
Three Manure Forks.
Set Beam Scales and Weights.
Manure Hook and Drag.
Two Grafting Tools.
Pick and Mattock.
Axe, Hook, and Mittens.
Pair of Hedge Shears.
Four Hammers.
Cross-cut Saw.

Sale at School Clough Farm, Longnor, October 29th,

Pig Bench.
Joiner's Bench.
Iron Pig Trough.
Three Wood Pig Troughs.
Two Wood Sheep Racks, on wheels.
Three Scythes.
Three Ladders (in Lots).
Sheep Rack on wheels.
Heel Rake.
Ditto.
Quantity Hay Rakes and Forks (in Lots).
Wheelbarrow.
Winnowing Machine.
Cake Crusher, in good order.
Chaff-cutter, in good order.
Set Chain Harrows.
Set Iron Seed Harrows.
Set Wood Harrows.
Martin's Spring Cultivator.
Wood Plough, by *Cooke.*
Iron Cylinder Land Roll, in good order.
Nicholson's Horse Rake.
Tedding Machine, by *Bamfords,* in good order.
Swath Turner, by *Bamfords,* nearly new.
Two-horse Mower, by *Hornsby's,* nearly new.
Two-horse Mower, by *Burgess,* in good order.
Reaping Tackle for two-horse Mower.
Ditto for Single Mower.
Pair of Light Wheels.
Pair of Cart Wheels, Iron Arms, and Sideboards.
4½ inch, Cart, with Sideboards, Wraithes, and Gormers, complete.

By Coalpit Lane 1939.
Phyllis Beresford, Charlie Gilman and baby John, George Beresford, Eric Oliver, Gladys Beresford.

Irish labourers haymaking at Boosley Grange.

Ben Mellor and Jack Kirkham stooking sheaves.

AROUND THE OAKENCLOUGH VALLEY (Claude)

The Oakenclough valley is mainly in the parish of Heathylee. The brook was known as the Ardenn Brook until around the 1600s. The parish starts at the ford on the River Manifold between Waterhouse farm and Over Boothlow and runs west towards Middle Hills.

Waterhouse is well named because of the good fresh water supplies there. Watering places can be seen in the yard and in the fields bordering the track; holding their flow in the dry times of summer and the frozen days of winter.

We now come up to and cross the old Brierlow Bar to Cheadle road, turnpiked in 1770. From here the ridge begins to rise from the Manifold towards Longnor Wood. The next farm is Heath House and below that are the remains of a lime kiln and a brick kiln with Longnor Mill below again. From Heath House, we can follow the 1765 turnpike road to Hardings (Hardens, 1658 parish register, Ardenn?) Booth. This road was developed further when Josiah Wedgwood needed a reliable route to transport chert, a very hard form of limestone used in the pottery industry, from Longstone Edge, near Hassop to the Potteries. Prior to that it was an old hollow way, sections of which can still be seen on the left. It was known as Jaggers Lane at Hardings Booth and would have been used by pack horses carrying salt, cheese, grain, chert, wool etc.

Hardings Booth was originally a vaccary where cattle were kept. At one time it was the major settlement in Heathylee. The remains of Heathylee House are about half a mile up the Manifold on the hillside.

An old packhorse way left the turnpike and continued a short way to Shining Ford where there was a blacksmith and wheelwright until the 1960s. There was also a pub called the Blue Bell. Here was a junction of paths, some now lost; the road past now is known as Coalpit Lane, probably because that was the road used to go to the coal pits. On the crossroads above there is an old stone building which was an early school. The track to the left here leads back to Longnor passing the remains of an old lime kiln. This was part of the old Leek to Longnor pre-turnpike road.

The limestone was carried by pack horses to where the lime was needed for the land or for mortar for building, and timber was readily available as the woodland was cleared for farming. Later on coal was used to burn the lime, but the lime-ash was not as good for the land as that burnt with wood. If you notice, all these lime kilns were near to pack horse routes. Limestone was a good return load on the east-west routes; salt from Cheshire, west to east and

Joe Belfield, lime spreading near the Roches.

any return load that could be found was carried.

Lime itself was difficult to carry being highly volatile; if it got wet it could be dangerous and needed very good panniers. Limestone is quite safe but very heavy. When the lime was drawn out of the kilns, the small lime and the ash together were beneficial to the land immediately, but the big lumps were put on one side and left to 'fall' or put in a container like a churn and water added. This is called slacking or slaking. After about two minutes the lime and water react violently, boiling up and getting very hot. When left, perhaps for a couple of weeks, the water is drained off and the lime underneath is like putty, ready for whitewashing or making mortar. The lime left to fall, when the weather has done the work, finishes up powdery and was spread from horse and cart or sledge on hilly land.

One old trail from Shining Ford went towards Oakenclough past a set of water troughs, which still exist, then past Oakenclough Manor and near to Hocker Farm to join the Marnshaw (Mountshaw) Head Lane and on towards Washgate or Hollinsclough.

Another trail left Oakenclough and went towards Middle hills fording the brook by an old clapper bridge, then passing Edge End, which has now gone and then Savage Croft with its chapel, also now gone; past Boarsgrave and then Row Ridge, also gone and joining onto the existing road near to the now restored water trough.

At the bottom of Oakenclough yard, we found an underground chamber, which is more than 23 feet deep and made of small old-fashioned bricks. We thought that it might be an ice-house. It is at the side of the site of old fish ponds, so the ice would have been available to store and being on a junction of pack horse ways, carriers would have been able to replenish their ice if carrying perishable goods like fish.

As with other big farms along the pack horse routes, cattle urine was collected to be taken away in barrels which were loaded onto the pack horse panniers to go for distilling for the ammonia and saltpetre for tanning leather, fulling cloth and manufacture of explosives. In the shippons there are stone troughs, now covered, which collected the urine. In the yard was a big stone water trough with a fountain, which was sold about 30 years ago by a previous owner.

Cheese and butter would have been made; when we came here, there were the remains of a big cheese press and the plant, rumex alpinus, commonly known as monk's rhubarb or butter dock was cultivated to wrap butter in, it being of a greaseproof nature, folding easily, non-poisonous and being available from May to November when there was the flush of milk to be processed.

When the cheeses were ready for selling, with their hard crust after curing, they would be taken to Longnor to be weighed and graded ready for sending on to other markets. They would be despatched along with other people's on a packhorse cheese train. Smaller lots might have gone to the Cheshire Cheese in Longnor - they were cheese dealers - and sorted and weighed for local markets. Butter would go to the buttermarkets at Leek, Macclesfield and other local markets.

Back to the trail heading for Middle Hills; when we arrive at the ridge road our way goes right towards Royal Cottage. The ridge road (moor ridge, Morridge) would be an important road before the Romans came. There has been an inn at Royal Cottage for many years, though it used to be on the opposite side, which is now a cowshed, but you can see the traces of front door and windows. Folklore says it is so called because of its association with Bonnie Prince Charlie, though some think it debatable if he stayed there.

Jim Beswick Snr and Jim Beswick Jnr, Gamballs Farm, Quarnford.

We now take the road to Longnor over Bare Leg Hill; so called because Stalks Heath - a kind of heather grows on the hill and after the leaves have fallen the stalks look like chicken leg bones and were collected for fire-lighting. Others have said the name comes from the Scotsmen lifting their kilts! Then we pass the snow stones to guide travellers as to where the road was in deep snow.

Near to where a track comes down from the left is a piece of land which was kept for growing potatoes for eating and for seed, free from disease and blight at that altitude. Fresh seed every year helps to prevent disease.

Next is Ridge Head with plenty of good water, then Merrill Grove, and nearby are the ruins of a thatched cottage last lived in in the 1930s by the Lane family. In the past it was used as a skin and bone yard. Next we come to Hocker farms with Badger's Croft down to the right, built on the junction of several streams. First documented as a hamlet in 1333, the name is thought to have developed from the name of the owner, Bochardes. Badger is also the name of a pedlar who carried his goods on his back and one or two pack horses. These men sold from farm to farm or village to village, 'badgering' people to buy, sometimes against their will. These were totally different from packhorse men, who were point to point carriers. The badgers or pedlars (roaming salesmen) used Badger's Croft for food and shelter from the weather; blizzards were common on the high moorlands.

As we carry on east down the road towards Longnor, next we come to Barrow Moor, an old hamlet with a hostelry, where packhorsemen got refreshment and bed for the night. In some parts of the country, it was the custom to have a branch of holly hung outside to show that accommodation was available, which gives rise to the name, Hollybush Inn. What little profit was made out of the job was used to buy any surrounding land.

Another 300 yards down the road, we come back to Hardings Booth. On the left is an old yew tree and opposite is where the Oakenclough brook joins the River Manifold. Further on is the sluice which controls water into the mill race and mill pond. Then past the mill and onto Longnor Bridge, near to where we started.

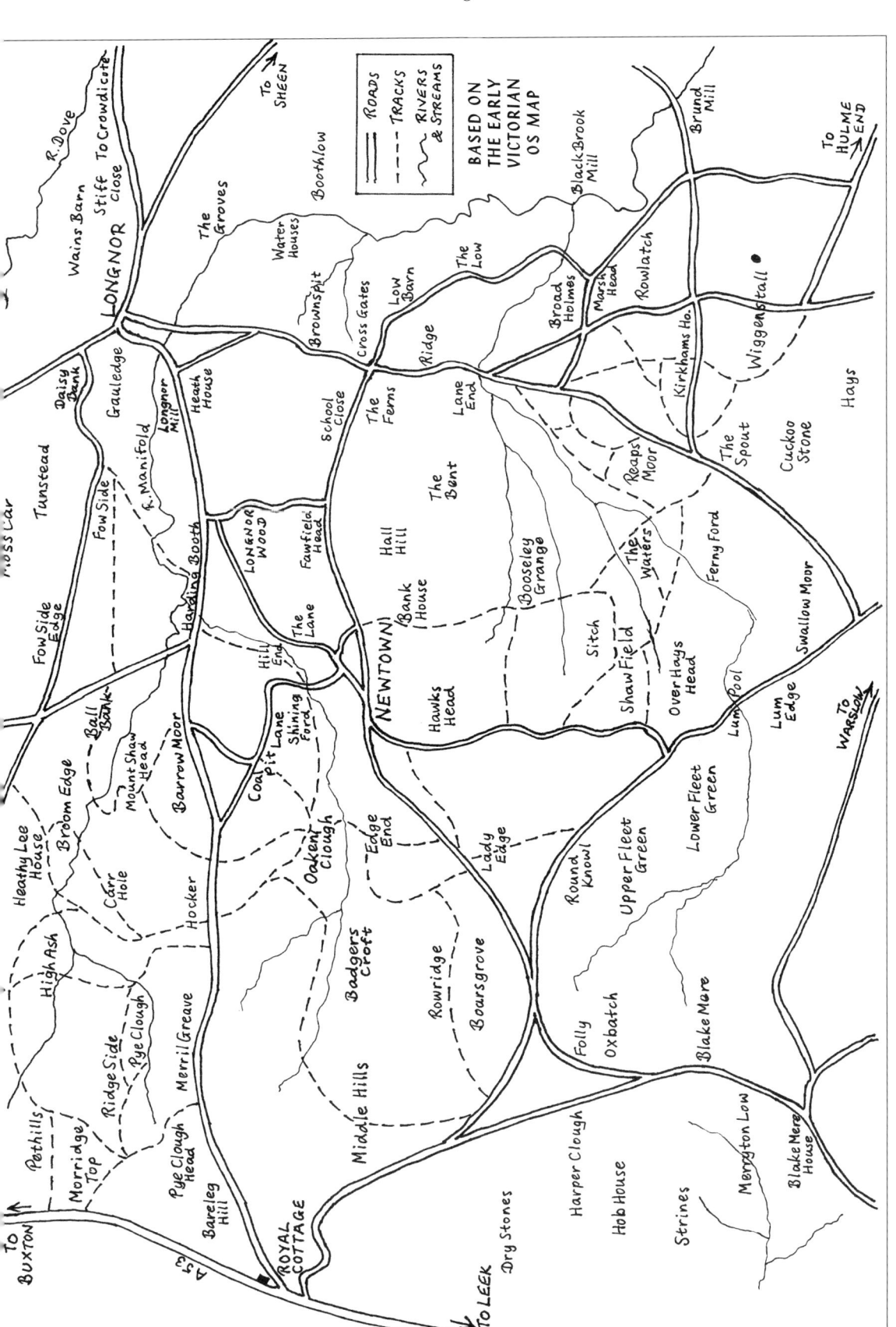

BASED ON
THE EARLY
VICTORIAN
OS MAP

ROADS
TRACKS
RIVERS & STREAMS

John S. Mellor

I was born at Belfield House, Newtown. When I was 18 months old we moved to Hardingsbooth, where Dad, Ben, was tenant until 1946, when he bought Fawfieldhead Farm. I can remember the American army being across at Ball Bank and Dad taking them a couple of buckets of milk across and bringing back a bucket of sugar which was very valuable then.

We normally fetched water from Walter Cundy's yard, but that would dry up in the summer, then I used to go with my mother across the fields to fetch it from a spring as the river water wasn't fit to drink.

We walked to Newtown school along Coalpit Lane. I've an idea it was called that because it was the way folks went to the coal pits around Flash. As we came back we'd stop at Shining Ford smithy and Mr Bradbury would let us pump the bellows to hot the fire to make the horseshoes.

Mrs Berrisford from Hocker farm would walk across the fields in all weathers to the school to light the stove. She'd be there by half past seven and it would be warm for us by 9 o'clock. She had about 10s a week for that. In winter we took potatoes with our initials carved on top and put them on the stove and had baked potato at dinnertime.

I remember all the older women seemed to wear long dark-coloured clothes and have a hessian sack apron. Old Harry Sleigh used to live across at Marnshaw and he was walking to Longnor one day in the early 1940s. There was a snow and Dad said to mother, *'When 'e comes back, give 'im summat t' eat', a*nd he ate a full apple pie, got up and walked round the table a few times, then sat down and ate half an egg custard. He frightened my mother, she thought he was going to have a fit. She went mad after, 'cus he'd eaten most of what we'd got as there was rationing on at the time.

In March 1940, Dad was going to Reapsmoor factory, taking the milk with the motor, an Austin 12 and trailer and there was a blizzard on. He met the mail van and crashed - neither could see the other. The winter of 1947 we were living at Fawfieldhead. Dad and Dick Keeling dug to the hay shed in the field for three days before they got any hay back for the cows. It took all day to dig to the shed and by that time it was too late to get the hay and then overnight it filled it in again. It was like sand blowing, you could walk over the walls anywhere. I remember a gang of men ridding the roads that came down to have a brew at dinnertime and one hadn't much to bring, so he brought a dozen hard-boiled eggs and ate them and a pan-sod - a scone made in a frying pan. I don't think he would be fit for much work after that.

When Dad was 9 years old, he went from School Clough to Longnor with his father, Clement, on horseback, and coming back, near to Brownspit, Grandad got off the horse to walk up to Foxhole barn to feed some cattle there and sent Dad home on the horse. But Dad couldn't stop the horse; it went up School Clough lane full gallop to where men were snow-ridding. One of them, Jim Storer, lay down across the road thinking it would stop the horse; but it went straight over the top of him and didn't stop till it got into the yard.

In the winter of 1953, I came back from Buxton School early on the 1 o'clock bus with Dennis Howson, who lived with his sister and her husband, and it was filling the road up; it was like a vacuum, the wind was blowing over the top and we had to walk backwards up the lane. A day or two later a Fordson tractor and snowplough were buried; they had to dig a snow ramp so that it could be driven up and into the field.

1963 was another bad winter. I took our milk and Dick Keeling's down to Reapsmoor Cheese factory with a little grey Fergie and transport box through the field for weeks. It froze the air line under the yard, so we had to roll a pipe out for the vacuum to milk the cows, then roll it up and put it away again after milking. It was June in odd places before the water came free, it had frozen that far underground.

There was a cattle sale at Warslow, I think it was Mottrams, on a Friday monthly during the summer at the back of The Greyhound. There were cattle pens and around 40-50 cattle there. In April 1957, I remember walking from Fawfieldhead with three heifers for the Sale. When we got to Newtown school, one jumped over a wall and made a dash for home. So Dad left me with the other two to carry on for Warslow and he went back where he turned two more out to the one that had galloped home, and followed on. At Warslow, he sold the intended three and I had to walk back with the other two. The Suez crisis was on and you could drive a car with L plates without anyone with you because there was fuel rationing, so Dad said, *'when you get back with those two, get the car out and fetch me.'*

My Grandad on my mother's side, Jim Oliver, came from Annroach at Quarnford. He had a neighbour with a hencote and Grandad used to see him going to it with a bucket. He thought it was funny that he'd never seen any hens, so one night he decided to have a look. He sneaked across and looked in, the cote had no floor in, but there was a ladder going down a hole. He was fetching coal, which wasn't allowed without a license or if you were a tenant.

Grandad Mellor had a hencote and the neighbour put an empty cote over the wall with straw in the nest-boxes. The hens went and laid in his shed, and back to eat and sleep in Grandad's.

I started travelling in 1967 for Delsanex, selling dairy detergents, but they sold out to Diversey in 1968 and I was made redundant. I was contacted by Massey's Feeds and have been with them ever since. Their depot in Longnor is the only one left in the area now. When I started, there were Staffordshire Farmers at Millers Dale, Criddles at Hartington, Manchester and Macclesfield Farmers at Chapel-en-le Frith and Cauldwells at Hulme End. The Longnor depot was purchased from Thomas Belfield in 1946 and was run under the name of William Loose & Co (Welco) as part of Massey Brothers (Cranage) Ltds, later Massey Bros (Feeds) Ltd.

When I started all corn was delivered in bags, but in 1970 when bulk corn was introduced it was delivered in unsewn bags on a wagon with a hopper on the back and the bags were tipped into the hopper and blown onto a loft or into the bin on the farm. It was a minimum of two ton lots and you got £1.50 a ton discount. Rolled barley was £28 a ton and dairy cake £37/£38 a ton. I have an invoice from W. Loose in 1921 showing Indie meal at £20/21 a ton. In the early 1930s, when Donald Ramsden was travelling, he told me it was down to £7 a ton.

I've seen many changes over the years; I think milk quotas affected us most at the time. Sales dropped 14% overnight as farmers cut back and it was a long time before things settled down.

Mid-1970s

Tommy Gould, Charlie and
Linda Mellor and John
Gould on top of the Fordson
Major and snow plough.
1953 winter.

RIGHT
John Mellor, Uncle Charlie and
Linda Mellor near Brownspit.

Below, snow-ridding in Low
Lane 1963.
L-R: Eric Garnett, Henry
Mycock, Clive Garnett, John
Sutton, Gilbert Lownds

Cliff Wardle

New Years Day at Longnor, they had 'Gorby day'. All these farmers used come to hire a worker and they gave you a shillin' hirin' money and you were fast for that year. Your wage 'ud be 5 bob a wik, that'd be £13 a year. George Horobin told me. Instead o' wearin' a slop, y'ad like a nightgown wi' pockets and the lads stood on Longnor Market place waitin' to be hired. Old George says t' this bloke, *"Ave yer got a good table?"* 'E says, *'It's oak 'en.'* *'It dunna matter about oak 'en, dus put any grub on it!'*

I can just remember th' cattle pens, I'd be about 6 or 7 when they took them out. I was born in 1920 at Underhill - Woodbine, next t' th' Yew Tree. I went workin' for Grindeys there, them as owned it; 5 bob a wik an' no woman in th' house. I've sit down there an' milked 25 beese of a mornin' on me own, cus 'e never got up 'til dinnertime - 'e liked a drink. Then take th' milk t' th' factory at Glutton, get back, take th' 'orse out an' feed 'er. It could be 10 o'clock before I got to slash some off the ham t' eat.

The cheeses from Glutton were well wrapped, a lot o' baggin' round 'em. We'd 'ave one about 18lb and roll it between milk churns an' jam it, because float bottom were dirty. Ee, they were good cheese an' yer didna bother about any dinner if yer'd 'ad a good feed o' that.

There used be annual sheep wash at Crowdicote. Farmers came from Monyash an' Flagg an' all round with horse and float, and any weak sheep, they used stick 'em in the float t' take back. They'd give us lads half a crown to fetch a gallon o' ale from the Packhorse - half on 'em went back boozed up. Little Jack Mellor from Longnor lost 'is sheep, 'e were so drunk.

There were a very big 'bobby' at Longnor, and Little Jack were a begger to fight, an' this bobby tried t'arrest 'im. So what Jack did, 'e ran an' bobby run after 'im, then 'e turned round an' shot 'is 'ead between bobby's legs an' tipped 'im over t' top on 'im. And when it come t' court in Leek, Judge said t' th' bobby, 'What! A little man like that knocked you down?' 'Yes.' He got summonsed half a crown for knockin' bobby down.

There was a mill at Crowdicote; old George Horobin used t' grind corn, but it all fell int' decay when people gave over ploughin' and growin' their own corn. Horobins were farmin' the Meadow Farm then; they bought it off the Duke. Round there were Wardles, Cundys, Bagnalls, Grindeys, all cousins. At the smithy, Stephen Gregory's mother was a Wardle, our great aunt Ann. The Bank, on Crowdicote bank, was a tiny cottage - Dad was born there; there were 10 children.

Billy Bills was a butcher in Buxton. His mother was my great aunt Sarah Wardle. She used go out wi' meat, wi' horse an' trap, she could be up Flass sellin' meat at midnight. She 'ad a sister up there, 'ad about 7 children. She said to 'er one day, 'I'm gooin' tak that lad.' That were Walter Wardle; an' 'er took 'im in a

Granny Wardle at The Bank 1920s.

The Grapes.

Mrs Horobin's,
Crowdicote, Longnor.

Edwin Wheeldon shoeing Sam Slack's horse next to the Horseshoe at Longnor c.1920.

clothes basket, wrapped up in a blanket so 'er son Billy 'ud 'ave a mate. They were cousins yer see. 'They'll grow up 'gether' 'er said. They learnt Walter 'is trade, pork butcherin' an' then when 'e were owd enough an' got married, they set 'im up on Cheese Hill with a butchers shop.

In Longnor, opposite Cheshire Cheese, where th' council houses are now, there were a croft an' a wall divided it; Crewe and Harpur property on one side and Cheshire Cheese th' other. Them at th' Crewe, the two Miss Gould spinsters fell out wi' Mrs Robinson as kept the Cheese; so they put a big sign up facing Crowdicote, uptown, advertisin' the Crewe and Harpur Arms. So Mrs Robinson 'ad one written out as well - Charlie Mellor 'e did sign writin' - and put up over the wall. So this went on for a while and nobody spoke. Well, there was a trick done, I won't say who was involved. It had to be done quick - four men and four pieces o' ladder - unscrew the signs and swap 'em over. Well; there were 'ell-up again.

We were stood under th' Horseshoe end, natterin', where we used meet, all th' lads. Bobby used come down an' say, *'Are yer behavin' or should I tell yer t' move on.'* We only used go round back o' th' Horseshoe an' come back agen an' 'e never bothered no more.

Owd Charlie Mellor come to us. *'I want thank yo lads.'* 'Why d'yer want thank us Mr Mellor?' *'Well; some o' yous among it; yer found me a job an' it paid well. Here's 2 shillin'; go in there an' buy half a gallon o' beer, get a glass o' two off Fred and get it drunk.'*

There were a lot o' poachers in Longnor at one time; a lot 'ad a runnin' dog an' went after rabbits, hares an' that. Ginger Bill and Thompsons got caught on Fawside, ferretin', by Slack the gamekeeper. Cost 'em 7 shillin' a piece and they were ordered t' destroy the dogs. So what they did was send 'em t' somebody else an' put whitewash on 'em an' bring 'em back as different dogs. They never got shut on 'em.

They used go on Dove Bonk as well. Owd Bony was keeper there; Heathcote from Earl Sterndale. 'E got little Tommy Thompson ferretin' an' 'e got 'im 6 months in jail on the treadmill. Tommy told me this - that were a belt where they used grind corn an' yer 'ad keep walkin' t' keep it goin'. 'E said it were 'ard work t' pull this big wheel round, Thee were buggered be nate, I'll tell thee! Wife were left wi' two children an' nowt t' eat i' th' 'ouse. 'Er managed get a bit o' scrubbin' er weshin' for somebody for a shillin' o' two.

They gen 'im half a crown t' come out o' jail with, an' a pass t' Buxton on the train. Walkin' back, 'e met owd Bony. *Well thee got me i' jail, and last letter I 'ad from th' wife, she'd nothin' t' eat i' th' 'ouse; so I'm goin' on Dove Bonk t'nate an' I'm goin' t' get a rabbit; I'm goin' t' feed them children. An if tha comes near me, I'll knock thee neck out; so keep away if tha sees me. An' this half crown, when I get t' Longnor, I'm getting' a tin o' tomaters an' some bacon.'* And when 'e got back, she put 'er arms round 'im and there were tears in 'er eyes when she saw the food. Owd Bony were theer, watchin, but 'e never come near an' he got 4 rabbits an' went an' seowd two for a tanner a piece.

Little Tommy only 'ad one eye, 'e'd lost one in Earl Sterndale dale, gettin' stone. 'E used get it an' break it an' the council used buy it off 'im fer th' roads. They used call 'im Caddy cus 'e used wear a black cad over 'is eye. Me Grandfather Turner lost an eye getting' stone in that quarry; it belonged t' Miss Finney. And the other quarry past Glutton Bridge up to Sterndale; me father's uncle Jack lost an eye there.

Father's uncle Tom was a railway engineer. 'E were a big feller and they called 'im Hoppy Tom cus 'e'd 'ad 'is leg broken and 'e hopped along. They were driving the tunnel from Hindlow t' Dowlow; it were all hand-drilled then. 'E 'ad a lot o' Irishmen workin' for 'im; some were killed. They 'ad huts in them fields at Hindler, that big field goin' down t' Brierlow Bar, full of Irishmen an' their wives. Uncle Tom were born at Brierlow Bar; there were a toll-bar there and cottage, and one at Glutton Bridge. Father's granny used keep toll-bar at Crowdicote. Across theer were two gates, same as at Glutton and Hindler.

Th' Irishmen didn't turn up one Monday mornin' and uncle Tom 'ad horse and trap and went t' Quiet Woman at Sterndale. 'E said, *I'll buy yer all a pint a piece an' if the's any bugger not out o' this place in 10 minutes, I'll thump the bugger out.'* One Irishman stood up. *'I'll take you on Tommy.'* *'Right, you're the man!'* This chap as were tellin' me, Ern Bagshaw, said, *'Tommy did thump 'im, an' after 'e'd say, 'Oh, keep out o' the way o' Tommy, 'e's a fightin' man!'* Some times they'd be drunk an' thrashin' their wives an' Tommy 'ud be sent for t' bail 'em. 'E used stick 'is foot in their behind, 'Bugger off work!' They said 'e was a cruel man to work for, but 'e paid well.

Me grandmother kept Islington; it were a pub at one time, then made inter a lodgin' house. Me grandfather, Mark Wardle, came from Dove Head. They reckon 'ow these Wardles landed at Flass, there were a lass got inter trouble with one o' these Dukes. Mary Wardle and they sent 'er up ter Brandside with a cow and calf, a pig an' some hens. They paid for this lad to be educated an' 'e did very well. They were rum fellers, these Wardles; if they saw a nice lookin' girl, they'd say I'm 'avin' 'er an' they used take 'er.

A Wardle invented that machine that they made ther own money with an' when this bloke come int' th' house they showed 'im some. *'What do you think about it?'* An' instead o' sayin' it looked nice 'e says, *'It looks flash dunt it?'* An' that's 'ow it got its name, Flash Money. They used t' deal with their own money between theirselves.

When the war started, I was called up and went in the Light Infantry. I ended up in the trenches machine gunnin' at Anzio beachhead, below Monte Casino and instead of the barrage; our own guns dropped it among us. You see the guns had been in North Africa and they were worn out, they don't shoot as far. A 25 pounder dropped and blew us up; it came spinnin' down, I can't remember it hittin' the floor. That's what gave me neurosis - bomb happy the soldiers called it. I can tell thee, when I come round, there were four Italians swingin' me on a blanket. They chucked me where dead were all stacked up, an' wounded were lyin' groanin. I thought, this is a rum bloody place t' come to!

Cliff Wardle

I thought I'd pee'd meself, but it were blood runnin' inter me boot. I'd got a dressin' in me back pocket, but it werena big enough t' go on this wound; it were 8 inches long an' 4 wide, rate across me guts. It 'ad split buckles on me greatcoat an' me back were splattered wi' shrapnel - I'm still pullin' it out.

So I got me gas cape an' put that round an' it were 6 weeks before I could get Germans look at it. After I kept complaining they took a look at it. *'We're going to take this shrapnel out; get on the bed. We haven't much anaesthetic for prisoners. Count up to 20 and you'll be asleep.'* I could have counted to 120 and not been asleep. They tied me hands behind me with a towel and they tied me feet and never even took me tunic off. 'Is mate 'eld it up an' 'e went in with bloody scissors an' pulled it out - four lumps an' put 'em in me top pocket. They stuck us on train from Florence to Munich, through Brenner Pass. We were in railway carriage with nowt only a beer barrel to pee in and when you stopped at a station, tip it out.

When the next doctor looked at me wound, he said, *'Do you know who's saved your life?'* 'No.' *'Those little friends you've got there; maggots; they've eaten the bad flesh out of it.'* It was like a piece of raw liver. *'Go into that room.'* And 'e says to the German guard, *'Take him to the shower and let the hot water run in as hot as he can stand it.'* We'd never 'ad a wash for weeks. I went back to 'im. *'It looks much better now.'* He spoke good English. *'I've sent your clothes to be gassed, you won't have any more trouble with your little friends now.'* We were lousy; we'd been shut in some barns as Russians 'ad been in, we'd none before that.

Next mornin' I was taken to a big fine house. There were 300 wounded Germans on top, and in the bottom women stemmin' grenades; puttin' 2 second an' 4 second fuses in 'em. They opened the winders when they see'd me. 'Englander?' 'Ja.' They wanted t' know all about the war; they knew nowt. Wanted t' know if I'd got a Frau. 'Nay.' 'Komm mit, komm mit!' - they were full of fun. There, I saw another doctor. *'Have they dressed it?'* 'Yes.' *'What part of England do you come from?'* Well, you'd to be careful. *'Between Manchester and Derby.'* I replied *'Do you know Manchester well?'* 'Yes.' *'Do you know the skin hospital?'* *'Yes, Key Street, Salford. I worked in the lime kilns and got dermatitis and went there for treatment.'* *'Who did you see?'* *'DP Mountford.'* *'I know him well, I did my skin training under him and went to his house for Sunday tea many times. If I give you a letter, would you take care of it and try to drop it to him when things are over.'* Which I did.

I was on camp staff for 3

Thomas Robinson, and son and daughter, of the Cheshire Cheese c.1910.

months while the wounds healed. As a POW, I'd no need to work, but I did some in a brick and tile factory. We had to cut our britches legs off t' make shorts; sweat were runnin' off us as we fetched the hot slates out. Wagons an' tracters an' trailers were comin' for 'em, they were in big demand. There were a bullock there; they used fetch clay out o' the pit wi' it. I got an owd sweepin' brush an' some soap powder an' give 'im a good wash. He'd got long feet curling and I got them up onto a log and got an axe an' chopped a bit off the front. The boss of the factory came over; 'e 'ad a big beer belly and chops full o' gold teeth. 'E'd bin watchin, *'Vot is your name?' 'Cliff.' 'I've never seen Charlie look so good. I saw you trimming his feet and he looks white. You are very good man with Charlie.'* And 'e gave me two cigars about a foot long; I cut 'em up an' smoked 'em in me pipe later.

My base camp was Stalag VIIIC near Breslau. They wanted volunteers t' go t' Breslau post office t' sort stuff comin' back from the Russian Front from the dead soldiers and stuff goin' out for Christmas. They gave us a Red Cross parcel t' share between two an' when we got there, they gave us another, but they stabbed it, so you had to use it, not hoard them for escapin'. The New Mills parcels were the best, they 'ad tinned sausage and bacon. There was egg powder as well, but the Germans wouldn't let us have that; they said it would cause TB. The prisoners who 'ad been there a long time, same as from Dunkirk; a lot o' them 'ad TB an' they said it 'ad come in the egg powder.

I once escaped; I was on a workin' party an' hung behind. I didn't get far, about 50 mile. I got an egg or two out of an 'en-cote an' caught a chicken an' plucked it, got a gallon tin an' some sticks, but couldn't make a fire 'less somebody see'd it. Then I fell asleep under a haycock an' I was found. They sent for an owd policemon; 'e'd bin retired, but they'd fetched 'im back cus th' young uns 'ad gone. 'E was like a fayther t' me, *'Komm mit, Clemence.'* He give me a bit o' thin twist; they called it 'kau-tabak' for chewin'. 'E put me in a cell, took me braces an' laces an' fetched me a blanket. I put me boots t' make a piller. Next mornin', 'e fetched me a drink o' coffee an' a piece o' bread an' butter. 'E were settin' garden, so I 'elped 'im. 'E went on duty, come back an' I were still 'elpin'. I were there 6 weeks; I used mop floor for th' owd woman. 'Er used boil me an egg; they were on ration as well, not a lot o' food; slice o' toast with a bit o' fat o' some sort. Anyway somebody reported 'im; seen me workin' without a guard an' they come an' fetched me back t' camp. Still, I got a 6 wik 'olidee out on it. If you were a country lad, it crippled you, paradin' round that same bit o' wire every day, round an' round.

Towards the end o' the war, they moved us out o' the road o' the Russians; they marched us 350 miles, a hell of a way. We slept under the stars and mostly, the only drink was what you could get, even from puddles. I 'ad no socks on. I did an old gypsy trick, you sleep in your boots an' every mornin', you walk in wet grass an' put yer boots straight back on, while they're still wet; I never 'ad a corn or a blister. Me socks were cripplin' me; I finished up with 'em like mittens. Some o' th' other lads were in a rum state wi' bleedin' feet.

Some o' them owd German women wi' their white hair in a bun at the back 'ud put a bucket o' water out for us. *'Wasser, gefangener* (prisoner).' And as we marched past, dip your tin mug in. But them SS guards were swines, one big fat bugger used kick the buckets ower. 'E'd shoot yer, soon as look at yer. I werena movin' fast enough one day an' a guard hit me with the rifle butt and broke my shoulder. I was knocked t' me knees an' couldna get up.

At the end, General Patten burst through the gates with tanks an' wagons; the guards scattered. We were livin' on flour an' warm water, they'd nothin' else t' give us. We'd all got dysentery, I was 6 stone when I got back an' could eat nowt. I was shakin' like a leaf. I tried for a war pension an' they gave me 7 an' 6 a week, same as a dog licence.

David Lownds

Our family came from Boosley Grange and we lived on a smallholding on Reapsmoor, Knowle Top. We had to carry water for drinking and washing from a little spring three fields away; clean it out then put one bucket under and fill it then another, every Sunday, ready for wash day. There was a little mere for the cows. In winter you hacked the ice off, but it gradually got less until there was nothing left and we had to carry water for them as well.

When the snow was on in 1947, I remember they dropped some bread and jam from a plane by parachute; Arthur Cope came round with it. Bill Cope used to charge the batteries up for the wireless. All accumulators were made of glass and were acid filled. Every week, depending on how much you used it, take it down to Moorside, below the Butchers Arms and everyone else took theirs too. He had a generator, there were wires and clips everywhere and everybody's batteries. You had your name on it but you might come back with someone else's or vice versa, it didn't matter. That was my job, to carry it across the fields; it had a little handle on.

Henry Prince, a neighbour, was the local pig killer, he used go round and kill pigs, then go back two days later and cut it up. He was also a cobbler. We used have a football, leather with a pig's bladder inside; he used mend it for us, putting patches on 'til it come to the state where he said there was no more room to put any on. We played the game one day and it went bang so we filled it up with grass to finish the game.

At Reapsmoor School, there was a black stove in the middle. One morning, Miss Cope the caretaker couldn't get it going, it was billowing smoke; we could hardly see anywhere. All at once a jackdaw shot out-half plucked. That was the highlight of the year.

We used to go to Sunday school in a morning, church in the afternoon and church again at night. One evening, there was a meeting to discuss where to go for the Sunday school trip, we all wanted to go to Skegness. We were waiting for Old Sam, one of the churchwardens. When he came Joyce said, *'The children would like to go to Skegness.'* *'Well,'* he said *'I can't see what's wrong with Trentham Gardens.'* And that was it, that's where we went.

There was an old gypsy caravan behind the Butchers Arms; friends of my Mum and Dad used live in it during the summer. He was a tinsmith from Redditch, Bob and Edith Bonser. He used make a lot of things for people, jugs and buckets.

The Lomas family at Cuckoo Stones, they used to have a 'Ministry' bull, a shorthorn and everybody from round used to take their cows to it because there was no AI then. The little building was on the side of the lane, Joe used go in and let him out and one or two of us 'ud stand topside and one or two bottomside. And after it'd performed, the old man used to say, *'That'll be half a crown.'*

There were always a few tramps about; Nobby, Congleton Bob and one called Jess. They used stop in the little hay barns or on the lofts; go from one farm to the other to cadge a bit o' porridge or summat. Of course, the biggest problem was matches and smokin'. Now and again a barn burnt down and you wondered what had happened. Old Tommy Phillips used to go round the farms with a big basket with boot polish, laces and stuff, once a month. He'd knock on the door and kneel on the step in a lot of cases. If he thought it was the right place, he'd get his mouth organ out and play a tune, a mass of foam round his mouth.

I was going to Warslow one night on my motorbike, and towards Eleven Lane Ends there was an old tip called Blackton tip and they used to dump surplus whey there from the cheese factories from time to time. It was a moonlit night with clouds passing; I saw this black

David, Graham and Brenda Lownds with Ken Mellor.

shadow moving across the road and thought it was a cloud. It was too late when I realised that it was a horde of rats as wide as the road and I was driving through them. I pulled my legs up I can tell you. They were making towards the tip; there must have been a few hundred. I'd heard old folks say about this kind of thing, but this night I saw it for real.

Bill Turner was from Cuckoo Stones above Lomas's and he worked for the council. His job was to keep the roads tidy from there to Sheen Church. He had a wooden wheelbarrow, two big brushes and a shovel and he kept it all clean and did the ditches. He also had two little Guernsey cows and a donkey. On a Sunday, he used harness this donkey up and fetch a churn of water to last him the week, which he filled from the trough at the bottom of the road about half a mile away. We were playing with a ball one day, a few of us lads. Old Bill was deaf and bending over getting the water. Our tennis ball hit the donkey in the ear and it set off up the road and tipped the cart over. Bill didn't know what had caused it, but because we were there, we got the blame. I used to help him haymaking with the donkey, but he wouldn't let me lead it, he said, *'Hup lad, it'll run away with you.'* It died eventually and old Bill said, *'It's done some tricks in its time, but it's never done one like that before.'*

Bill Turner.

Tom Bunting

When my mother, Annie Wood, lived at Dowel Hall just before the first war, she used to tell us that their neighbours, the Garnets at Glutton Bridge farm. used to go to Leek Fair and when they came back, they turned the cattle out regardless of the weather, 18th of May, that was turning out day. During the first war, the government moved them out of the farm and they went to Gotham farm, Pikehall. I think it was because explosives were being used experimentally nearby and it was thought too dangerous for them to be there. They had to go back for a year or two to draw compensation from the government.

Gwynne Floyd

In 1984 we semi-retired after my husband Arthur had health problems, and we moved to Reapsmoor to a smallholding known as Park House. On an old map it is marked as the Pound. It was a pig farm, but the buildings were quickly changed into suitable housing for horses; a passion of Arthur's. He was an engineer and had built horse-drawn vehicles previously; so after a couple of years, when his health had recovered, he built more vehicles. People were coming all the time; he schooled horses and taught people to drive them; folks from all over the country.

We organised a rally from Park House every year. We were members of the Staffs and Derbyshire group of the British Driving Society and during the summer, we would meet at pre-arranged venues and drive out. So we did this from Reapsmoor, often starting from John Mellor's field opposite and driving 12 to 14 miles with probably 15 to 20 turnouts. It was quite a spectacle; a very social occasion which we all looked forward to very much

All sorts of people from all walks of life and all age groups came to learn to drive. I remember someone coming from away, he came often; he was an academic and always consulted books about everything. He was out with Arthur one day driving a strong horse, but a safe horse. Going round Low Lane, the horse picked up speed and as they approached the main road, the learner started to panic. *'Arthur, Arthur, I can't stop him!'* Arthur replied, *'You must stop him, we're coming up to the main road.' 'I can't, I can't, what shall I do?'* And Arthur said, *'Read chapter 5, paragraph 14!'*

Arthur and Gwynne Floyd at Piggenhole Bridge.

Arthur died at Christmas 1997 and the following summer, I was asked if I would put on a drive in his memory, which we did. Drivers and friends came to take part in the occasion. We had 37 turnouts and many followers; what a tribute! It was very moving and a wonderful day.

Marjorie Mycock

When I was a child, the lads from Reapsmoor used to congregate around the school and I remember being frightened when they used to go down to Piggenhole Bridge and ride their bikes over the bridge wall.

Henry Mycock

When we were farming at Knowle House, Reapsmoor, I remember one day our neighbour had gone out with his horse and trap. After some time, this horse came trotting past and I saw there was no driver. The horse went past, turned round and went back to where he had set off from, trotting round the field with no driver. We heard later that the driver had 'disembarked' coming down Piggenhole Bank.

Marion Ashmore

'A CHILDHOOD AT CROTHCOTE': I was born at Toll Bar Cottage, Crowdicote, just before the war started. It was basically one up, one down, the bedroom divided in two and a tiny pantry, but the sink was in the house place. Luckily there was only me at home then; my brothers Cliff, Ike and Les were out in service or in the army and my sister, Doris was in service. She worked at the Packhorse, behind us, for Miss Maudsley, the landlady. It was very antiquated, but nice. They had a lot of well to do visitors. We were only allowed into the doorway for a bottle of pop and we had to return the bottle because there was a penny on it.

There were three girls in Crowdicote; Mary Chappel, Grace Sutton and myself. We played together and there was a family of Bradburys at Bridge End with quite a few boys. We used to get in trouble for putting snowballs down people's chimneys in the winter and making slides when it was icy. We had nothing much in the way of toys; our Doris bought me a secondhand doll and knitted clothes for it for Christmas and Dad bought a secondhand doll pram and painted it green.

I had a little Cairn terrier called Floss. She was born at Longnor, and Mr Thompson had these puppies in a little croft. We were going down to my Godmother's at High Acres that day, Mrs Gregory's, and we walked to Chesford bank (cheeseford) where she lived, and we saw these puppies and I wanted one of course. So Dad bought one and paid 3s 6d and I had her for my 7th birthday - she died on my 21st. Everywhere we went, she went; we dressed her up and put her in the doll pram and walked miles with her, she loved it. In the winter, she went sledging with us; we used to sledge from the top of Crowdicote bank, right down through the village, round the bends and over the bridge; there was no traffic then - we were little dare-devils. We went down a field at the back of the Packhorse one day and there were some cows there and Mary steered straight under this one's belly. I don't know who was the more frightened.

High Acres

We had a lovely time in the summer holidays; we used to sweep the shavings up in the joiner's shop for Mr Gregory and he gave us a couple of pennies. It was lovely in there, the smell of wood and he was showing us one day how he made dovetail joints. He was a wheelwright and used to repair farm carts and make coffins as well.

Marion's and Mary's
playhouse in the Mill.

Crowdicote Mill about
1920.

Below left
George Horobin at
Meadow Farm.

Below right
George and William
Horobin at Meadow Farm.

Then across the road to the Smithy where we used to sweep the parings from the horses hooves up, and blow the bellows when he was making the horseshoes. Then fetch the water to fill the container by the anvil for cooling them down. He had a cupboard with little drawers in full of nails which used to get mixed up, so we sorted those out too. Then weed round the outside and sweep that up and he gave us thre'pence.

We fetched the water from the standpipe and tap by the phone box. That was for the whole village; it came from the reservoir up between Earl Sterndale and Jerico. We used to weed and brush round there and clean the telephone box and put wildflowers in a jar in there.

In the snow of 1947, we didn't go to school for 4 or 5 weeks. I remember my Dad had a pair of clogs made for me. Bob Brough was the cobbler in Longnor. But they had rubber rinks on not metal, so they were quiet. We had a wonderful childhood; we'd got nothing but we'd got everything. We made play houses, Grace always had a 'hotel' and we went for lunch, like they did at the Packhorse. In the field down by the bridge was a little well called Fidget Well. The water came from the hill, Crowdicote bank, and it was always very cold, lovely, clear and fresh. On the Saturday of Buxton Carnival and Fair, we went along to that and then the next day, after Sunday School at Earl Sterndale, we decorated the well and had our own little well-dressing. We went out of the house early in the morning and never thought to come back home until tea time. Nobody worried about us, there was no harm.

Dad worked in the quarry at Dowlow. Mr Chappel worked at Hill Head Quarry and Grace's dad was a road sweeper over the River Dove in Staffordshire around Longnor and Sheen. Mr Horobin was our road sweeper on the Derbyshire side of the river. There were two old ladies down the lane, the Horobins. We got the sticks and coal in for Miss Patty. On bonfire night she did us an oven full of baked potatoes. Mam made treacle toffee and Mrs Chappel made parkin.

We loved sheep washing time; the farmers came down and damned the leat up which used to go to the old flour mill. They drove their sheep down from up on the limestone, Woolleys from top of Crowdicote, Mellands, Bradburys from High Needham, Broughs from Cronkston, people from Hurdlow Town and beyond. It went on for perhaps a week during our summer holidays. At lunchtime, the men went to the Packhorse for sandwiches and beer and we sat on a bank down the lane with a little stick each and kept the sheep there. There was some grazing and they used to give us thre'pence for tenting their sheep. There'd be half a dozen men, some stood in the water. They put some yellow stuff in part of it; they told us it was shampoo and the other part was clear water. It was all let back into the Dove, people didn't bother then but I never remember it killing any fish and there would have been trouble over the fishing if it had.

On a hot day, before Dad came back from work, mother would send me down to Fidget well with a little billy-can to fetch a pint of cold water for him to drink when he came home because the lime used to get in their throats. At the quarry, the stone was blasted, then men broke it and it was loaded on to horse and carts to be taken to the kilns. Later on they had a little engine on rails which they called a bogey. Dad drove it; the stone was put in wagons and it could pull more.

He worked at Dowlow for 54 years only missing a couple of days in the '47 snow, when he walked up the fields and over the top. When he finished on the Saturday, he walked with other men from Longnor over to Chelmorton to the butchers, Skidmores. When Mary and I were 12 or 13, there was a big snow and we took the big wooden sledge and sledged down Hindlow to Brierlow Bar and somebody in a bread van picked us up and took us to Buxton and we brought 26 loaves of bread back on the sledge in clean sacks. We sat on top of the bread and sailed back down towards Crowdicote with this bread for the village.

Mrs Sutton used to make wonderful currant bread which we took round to others in the village. Mam and Mrs Riley next door used to make plain bread; Mam would put it on a low chair in front of the fire to rise and put a cloth and tea towel over it and then an old towel. Invariably the cat would go and jump on it. They made oatcakes and when Cliff got married and lived across the valley at Under Whitle and kept a pig or two, I had to fetch the blood so that Mrs Riley and me Mam could make black puddings. They also made the most wonderful scratchings you've ever tasted after the fat was rendered. I fetched the blood in a white enamel bucket; walking across the fields - and *'keep stirring it with a wooden spoon and hurry up'* - over the bridge and up the lane, heaving me heart out. I've never liked black pudding - they said it was wonderful.

Country folk provided for the bad winters, they kept sacks of flour in and plenty of coal. We'd a few hens and Dad kept two gardens going, one opposite and one at the top of Crowdicote bank. That kept us going except when the gypsies decided to call and help theirselves, which from time to time they did. Mr Cundy who lived up the field caught them one day and gave them a right going over, so they didn't come for a year or two. Dad once went up and there wasn't a carrot or potato to be found, after all his hard work, walking to Dowlow every day and then to the top of the bank at night to the garden, us with him, and the little dog of course.

Dad played euphonium in Dove Valley band; we were naughty and used to put a little potato down it before he went to practice. The band practised on the loft at the Packhorse. They used to keep the music in a big box called the band box, like a trunk with a lid on. Mrs Goodwin was landlady then and she kept her potatoes on the loft. There was a funny smell one day and she was looking all round to see where it was coming from. She decided to lift the lid on the box. Well, there had been a local man missing for weeks and they had searched the river, which was a favourite spot for people to throw themselves in. This man had got drunk one night, gone up the loft and got down in this box and I don't know what happened, but the lid was down and he was dead. This morning, I remember my mother was scrubbing my face, when Mrs Goodwin came running down. *'Come quick-come quick! I've found ----.'* *'Where've you found him?'* *'Oh come with me, come with me, George's out.'* Anyway me Mam dumped me down and off she went. They came down from Longnor, old Charlie Mellor the undertaker and fetched him.

I've seen two bodies dragged out of the river. With one, Mary, Grace and I, we went across the Meadow lane which brought you out at Beggars Bridge and there was quite a deep whirlpool there. We used to pick primroses there. We sat behind the wall hidden because we saw the horse and cart coming and one or two men from the village with their drag forks. They dragged the river, got him out and put him on the cart and put a sheet over him. Another man went down his fields and drowned there and we watched them pull him out. So we were nosey kids - it was an exciting time for us. Dead bodies have never worried me.

When Cliff came home after being a prisoner of war, there was quite a gathering to meet him. He came on the 9 o'clock bus to Longnor, the last bus from Buxton. The vicar, Mr Gibson wanted to take him into the Horseshoe for a drink, but Mam wouldn't let him, he looked so ill and thin, like a clothes prop with clothes on. We walked home, Dad carried his kit bag and Mum put him straight to bed. Doctor Twigg came from Hartington the next day and said to mother, *'Don't go giving him any meat and potato pies or roast beef Mary. Get some porridge and milk puddings down him and that is all until I come again. Nowt else - if he wants it 'e conna have it.'*

Mother got him built up, then he went off for convalescence for 6 weeks and came back a lot better but he wouldn't talk about what he went through for years.

Crowdicote

William Bradbury Senr & Junr early 1950s. Bridge End Farm, Crowdicote.

The Toll Cottage at Crowdicote.

Crowdicote Smithy.

Joiner's Shop Crowdicote.

Sid Horobin of Crowdicote, Billy Wood of Upperhulme and Stephen Gregory of Hatchaway.

Mrs Horobin of Crowdicote.

Mary Wardle, and Marion and
Angela Ashmore.

At Bridge End Mary Bradbury
watched by her brothers and
sister in 1955.

Dove Valley Band 1910. L = Longnor. C = Crowdicote
BACK: W.H. Tunnicliffe L, Alfred Horobin C, Luke Gregory C, James Smith L, Mark Wardle C,
George Storer L, Herbert Thompson L, Thomas E. Gregory C, Stephen Gregory - Hatchaway (blacksmith),
James Cundy L (butcher), Charles Mellor L (undertaker).
FRONT: Thomas William Wardle C, Fred Wardle L (Horseshoe), Anthony Wilde - Mosscar,
Harry Milner C (Packhorse), Luke Gregory - High Acres Glutton, William Thompson L -Folds End,
John S. Gregory C (joiner/undertaker), John Mycock.

Quarry men at Dow Low, late 1940s.
BACK: Tom Prince, Tom Wood, Dick Dale, - Bramwell, Gilbert Armitt, Sidney Johnson.
FRONT: - -, Jack Brindley, Reg Armitt, Fred Hulme.

Mr and Mrs Wardle at the Toll House, Crowdicote

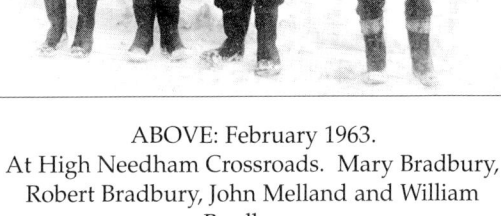

ABOVE: February 1963.
At High Needham Crossroads. Mary Bradbury, Robert Bradbury, John Melland and William Bradbury.

Mr and Mrs Turner, Marion and Cliff's grandparents, at The Ferns early 1900s.

Haymaking at Bridge End Farm, Crowdicote.

The 'Big Room', Earl Sterndale School 1948/9.
BACK: Edward Jenkins, Edwin Armitt, Janet Kidd, Gordon Booth, Derek Watson, Jean Gregory,
Mrs Weston, Beryl Gilman, Peter Turner, Ruby Hallowes?,Tony Calver, David Brindley.
KNEELING: Trevor Watson, Gordon Booth, Harry Hodgkinson, Pam Brindley, Peter Wardle?,
Ken Heathcote, Margaret Jenkins, Sam Bostock, Brian Brindley.

Earl Sterndale School early 1950s.

At Earl Sterndale

Earl Sterndale Church.

Emma Edge's Cottage, Reapsmoor.

Reapsmoor School 1955/56
BACK: John Lowe. Donald Lownds, Norma Holmes, Barbara Mellor, Brenda Lownds
MIDDLE: Joan Grindey, Maureen Cope, Mr Pearson, Hazel Lownds, Gwen Ball
FRONT: John Prince, Desmond Gee, Eileen Ball, Tony Gee, David Broomhead

The building on Reapsmoor that is now the church and the parish room was formerly church
and school and before that it was a workhouse. I was told that it was built by the Harpur-
Crewes and given to Fawfieldhead Parish for the care of the poor. The men and women were
kept separate. Any unmarried mothers had their children with them. They were only allowed
a certain amount of food; the mother had her ration and had to share it with her child. In one
of the record books it said that the unmarried girls could be hired out as servants to the
gentlemen of the parish *'to be done with as they willed.'* (Claude)

...and finally

Joyce and Jack Perkin.

George Critchlow at Sheen.

Wetton Mill.

Haymaking near Hulme End. John Bonsall on mowing machine.